A Space for Hate

The White Power Movement's Adaptation Into Cyberspace

By Adam G. Klein, Ph.D.

Litwin Books, LLC
Duluth, Minnesota

Published by Litwin Books, LLC, 2010
PO Box 3320
Duluth, MN 55803

http://litwinbooks.com/

This book is printed on acid-free paper that meets all present
ANSI standards for archival preservation.

Library of Congress Cataloging-in-Publication Data

Klein, Adam (Adam G.)
 A space for hate : the white power movement's adaptation into cyberspace / by Adam Klein.
    p. cm.
 Includes bibliographical references and index.
 Summary: "A study of the way hate groups, especially white supremacist groups, are using the Internet to spread their messages to a young
audience. Attention is given to the legal debate over hate speech and
free speech, and questions concerning ethics and rhetoric in the Internet
space"--Provided by publisher.
 ISBN 978-1-936117-07-9 (alk. paper)
 1. White supremacy movements. 2. Hate groups--Computer network
resources. 3. Hate speech. 4. Freedom of speech. I. Title.
 HV6437.K54 2010
 320.5'6--dc22
                                 2010007056

A Space for Hate

For Meryl and Peter

Acknowledgements

A special thanks to Professor Anju Chaudhary, Professor Barbara Hines, and Professor Carolyn Byerly of Howard University's Mass Communication & Media Studies Graduate Program; Rory Litwin and the team at Litwin Books; and Allison, without whose support this project would not have been possible. And to Peter Klein, my "editor-in-chief."

Contents

Introduction

June 10, 2009: James von Brunn logged off his Packard Bell computer, grabbed his keys and strode out the door of his son's Annapolis apartment. He had moved in with his son and future daughter-in-law two years ago where he paid $400 a month in rent and spent most of his time on the Internet. The drive to Washington, DC was only 30 minutes from there, and 88 year-old James cruised along purposefully in his 2002 red Hyundai as he headed west toward the nation's capital. For a man approaching his 90s, the one time advertising copywriter, with a degree in journalism, was unusually media-savvy. Before leaving, he checked over the website he had launched for the purpose of selling a self-published book, and sent out a final email to inform his many readers that "they shouldn't expect to hear from him again."[1] James also made a few final notations in his notebook that now rested beside him on the passenger seat.

As he drove over the beltway and into the city, everything seemed in order, yet things were not quite right. James thought of the first black American president, Barack Obama, who just days before had made global headlines at a former Nazi concentration camp where he publicly denounced the growing wave of Holocaust deniers. From the president, his mind shifted to the economic recession that had taken away his livelihood, much as it had in 1981, when James took a similar trip to DC to visit then-Federal Reserve Board Chairman, Paul Volker. He felt little had changed since 1981. The real problem was not the recession or progressive politics. The real problem, underscored in his book, had always been the same – it was about the Jews. The newly scribbled pages of the notebook beside him summarized his beliefs. He wrote, "The Holocaust is a lie. Obama was cre-

---

[1] Darryl Fears and Marc Fisher. "A Suspect's Long History of Hate, and Signs of Strain." Retrieved July 20, 2009, from http://www.washingtonpost.com/wp-dyn/content/ article/2009/ 06/10/AR2009061003495.html?sid=ST2009061200050

ated by Jews. Obama does what his Jew owners tell him to do.
Jews captured America's money. Jews control the mass media."[2]

James double parked his car on the southbound side of 14th
Street next to the National Mall. He glanced long and decisively
at the entrance of the museum to his right. The clock on his
dashboard read 12:44pm. With that, he opened his driver side
door and reached over his notebook to grab a .22 caliber rifle.
When he approached the visitor's entrance of the U.S. Holocaust
Memorial Museum, the museum's security guard, Officer Stephen Tyrone Johns kindly opened the door for the old man.
James raised his rifle and shot directly into the chest of Johns, the
39 year-old African-American officer who had served as the museum's guard for six years.[3] From there, James tried to take his
firearm, and his rage, into the museum itself, which was filled
with visitors and a few Holocaust survivors on the premises that
day. The 88-year old man who had just shot Officer Johns in the
chest was stopped at the doorway by return fire from the other
guards. As he had told his ex-wife many times before, James was
attempting "to go out with his boots on."[4] Just after 1:00pm, the
lifelong white supremacist and anti-Semite, James von Brunn, lay
wounded and motionless on the floor of the Holocaust Museum
beside the African-American guard he had just shot dead.

The tragic shooting at the Holocaust Museum in 2009 was
not the first time that white power fanaticism has erupted into a
deadly shooting spree at the hands of one if its followers. In the
last ten years, there has been a violent strain of unhinged racists

---

[2] Theo Emery and Liz Robbins. "Holocaust Museum shooter James
von Brunn had history of hate." Retrieved July 20, 2009 from
http://seattletimes.nwsource.com/html/nationworld/2009330156_
holocaustshooting12.html

[3] United States Holocaust Memorial Museum. "In Memoriam." Retrieved July 20, 2009, from
http://www.ushmm.org/memoriam/detail.php?content=johns

[4] James G. Meek and Richard Schapiro. "Holocaust Museum shooter."
Retrieved July 20, 2009, from http://www.nydailynews.com/news/
us_world/2009/06/10/2009-06-10_holocaust_ museum_shooter
_james_von_brunns_exwife_says_his_racism_ate_him_alive.html

and white power ideologues that have turned their words of hatred into lethal acts of terror. In 2007 alone, the Federal Bureau
of Investigation reported that 7,624 hate crime incidents had
been committed across the United States.[5] According to their
statistics, almost every year both the volume and severity of these
incidents has increased. From Benjamin Williams, charged with
setting fire to three synagogues and killing a gay couple in California, to Benjamin Smith, whose own shooting spree through
Indiana and Illinois wounded eight targeted minorities and
claimed the lives of a Korean doctoral student and African-
American basketball coach. Unlike Williams and Smith, the most
recent high-profile assailant, James von Brunn, *had* been on the
FBI radar since his failed attempt to take the entire Federal Reserve Board hostage in 1981, claiming they were part of a larger
Jewish conspiracy. However, despite their differences in age,
background, and notoriety, von Brunn, Williams and Smith each
utilized the basic blueprint of the white power movement – racial
intolerance escalating into tirade, and hate speech graduating
into action. But these three murderers were tied by yet another
common thread that both documented and united their paths
along a global movement: the Internet.

   Like von Brunn who utilized his website, Holy Western Em-
pire, to publish his propagandist book, *Kill the Best Gentiles!*, Smith
and Williams also frequented the pages of white power domains
such as World Church of the Creator and Stormfront.[6] These
are the new Ku Klux Klan meeting halls, the latest Nuremberg
rally town squares. Only they do not take place in the backwoods
and basements of American subculture, and they are not adver-
tised in the swastikas and shields of the Third Reich. They are
websites, globally accessible to everyone via the World Wide
Web. Over the last decade, the white power movement has
steadily relocated its central base into the decentralized network

---

[5] FBI. "Incidents and Offenses." Retrieved July 20, 2009, from
http://www.fbi.gov/ucr/hc2007/incidents.htm
[6] Anti-Defamation League. Poisoning the Web: Hatred Online. (New
York: An ADL Publication, 2001).

of cyberspace; from hardcore skinhead gangs to the neo-Nazi party faithful. In this new virtual reality, Klan hoods have been replaced by a much thicker cloth of anonymity, and the book-burning rallies of yesterday have become today's white power music downloads, chat rooms, and picture galleries of online youth culture. But how did we get here so fast? When did the communication and recruiting strategies of America's racist un-derbelly become so proficient, professional, and even popular?

In fact, the concept of *mass mediated hate speech* is not a recent phenomenon. The paths to organized bigotry, hate crime, and even genocide have often been traced to a few embittered voices in a society brought together in larger numbers by the leading tools of the media of that society. History has revealed this in chillingly proficient ways. From Hitler's 1930s Nazi ferment that filled the pages of newspapers and bookshelves across Germany calling for all Jews to be cast from society, to the Hutu militia men in 1990s Rwanda, whose radio broadcasts prompted the mass murder of their fellow Tutsi countrymen and women. The relationship between hate speech and mass communication has steadily evolved together hand in hand with every new genera-tion, and the age of the Internet is no different.

Since 1995 when the first hate website was launched, until the present day, with over 10,000 sites currently operating across the web, the messages of intolerance and the primary mode for disseminating them have all gravitated onto the Internet. But unlike the other forms of communication used to deliver racist and anti-Semitic sentiments to the masses, the Internet has brought its own unique properties that not only transmit, but also transform, conceal, and seamlessly merge hate speech into the mainstream of popular culture. Most watchdog agencies firmly agree that the Internet, as a medium for white power objectives, has become the ideal "electronic venue that seems particularly suited for recruitment."[7] This book will examine how the Inter-

---

[7] Brentin Mock. "Sharing the Hate: Video-Sharing Websites Become Extremist Venue." Retrieved July 20, 2009, from http://www.splcenter.org/intel/intelreport/article.jsp?aid=756 (2007)

net, its structure, media properties and online trends, have allowed white supremacists to adapt all the communities of the
white power movement into one computer-screen-sized space –
shared by one billion users.[8]

A Space for Hate

A Space for Hate speaks to the media and information topic of
hate speech in cyberspace, but more specifically, how its inscribers have adapted their movement into the social networking and
information-providing contexts of the modern online community. While many studies in recent years have addressed the notable ways that popular Internet culture and cyber trends such as
blogging have democratized the community of information seekers and providers, little research to date has addressed the darker
element that has emerged from that same democratic sphere.
That is, the huge resurgence and successful transformation of
hate groups across cyberspace, and in particular, those that promote white supremacist ideas and causes. In 2009, hate speech
and white power movement organizations in the United States
are on the rise once again, fueled by new issues but with familiar
themes. Among them, the election of the first African-American
president of the United States, a national economic crisis that has
triggered ethnic scapegoating, and an immigration debate centered largely on illegal Hispanic immigrants. These are just some
of the emerging social issues by which today's hate groups have
framed familiar messages of blame, anger, fear, resistance, uprising and action.

This book will focus solely on the white power movement by
using hate-based websites as a concrete and measurable field for
examining racial and ethnically targeted messages in the age of
information and technology. Nowhere is this phenomenon more

---

[8] Rick C. Hodgin. "Internet becomes home to one billion people for
first time." Retrieved July 1, 2009, from
http://www.tgdaily.com/trendwatch-features/41166-Internet-
becomes-home-to-one-billion-people-for-first-time (2009)

widespread today than within the unguarded walls of cyberspace. The increasingly acceptable domain of anti-Semitic, anti-gay, and racist expression within such commonplace websites as Wikipedia, an information tool, and YouTube, the younger web community's digital hub, initially suggested the need to further research the way that cyberspace was allowing blatant hate speech to once again flourish within mainstream popular culture. That investigation has led directly to the sources themselves – white power movement websites – where readers of this text might be surprised to find hate speech being voiced through some of the most contemporary Internet features such as convergent multi-media centers, social networking forums, and perhaps most troubling of all, research and information tools.

For any website to reach and ultimately engage new members into its cause, both the community and the presentation of its message must identify with the qualities, needs, and desires of a target audience. For the white power movement, that new audience is clearly the white youth of higher education. In fact, that very goal is openly declared by many of the movement's leaders. Leaders like Matthew Hale, founder of World Church of the Creator, who states, "We generally reach out to the private colleges and universities...because we want to have the elite. We are striving for that, focusing on winning the best and the brightest of the young generation."[9] This study takes a deeper look into this process of attracting the "best and brightest" of the net generation by considering the white power movement's most recent adaptation into a model community of cyberspace; fully functional, informative, engaging, and user-friendly.

As a simultaneous exploration of those attributes that are unique to Internet youth culture, this book will also consider the ways by which the same traits have become the contemporary tools of the white power movement, enabling them to reconstruct

---

[9] Carol M. Swain and Russ Nieli. Contemporary Voices of White Nationalism in America. (Cambridge, UK: Cambridge University Press, 2003).

a more modernized message of hate. In the following chapters we will journey to the outer fringes of cyberspace to focus on three central pillars of hate speech on the Internet. They are the *legal and infrastructural framework*, which offers support to the white power movement, the *informational component*, which creates the illusion of academic legitimacy for the cause, and the *cultural context of cyberspace*, through which young users are constantly communicating, sharing, learning, and developing new ideas.

Chapter 1 will begin by examining a legal debate that has always surrounded the issue of hate speech in the public domain and is further being tested today on new ground amidst the World Wide Web. In the last decade, new mass communication concerns have arisen from the Internet, exclusively, that have indirectly affected the white power movement. Specifically, infrastructural issues such as the Internet's vast unregulated space, its decentralized and unaccountable host networks, and its limitless exposure to younger audiences are all areas that will be considered as the structural building blocks that, for now, benefit the inscribers of online hate speech. This chapter will also look at the ambiguity and challenges inherent in traditional hate speech legislation, such as the landmark case, *Chaplinski vs. New Hampshire*. Through the vagueness of such existing legislation, we can consider a legal definition of hate speech as something that the white power movement is keenly aware of – and carefully manages to avoid in the new cyber format.

From laws and infrastructure, chapter 2 will next examine the hazy relationship between information and propaganda online. This complex form of persuasive communication has steadily evolved over the years from preexisting strategies of hate speech, war-time rhetoric, and even politics. As a popular research base, the Internet is ideal for attracting and "educating" those information-seekers whom the white power groups most wish to recruit – college students. This section primarily addresses key theories of information, propaganda, and the media that have helped hate groups build a path to false knowledge on the Internet; what this researcher calls the process of *information laundering*. This new theory will demonstrate how the formats and constructs of cyberspace can act much like a system of money laundering by taking an illegitimate currency, in this case hate-based information, and transforming it into what is rapidly becoming acceptable web-based knowledge, thus washed virtually "clean" by the system. Through the model of information laundering, hate groups are entering into mainstream culture by attaining legitimacy from the established media constructs of cyberspace, primarily search engines and interlinking networks. These conventional paths can unwittingly lead an online information seeker to white power content that, as later research will show, has already been designed for them as being educational, political, scientific, and even spiritual in nature.

Chapter 3 will address what is perhaps the most important aspect of this subject, the cultural context of cyberspace. Here, we will identify the popular trends that have allowed hate groups to adapt and flourish often under the camouflage of a "user-friendly" social networking community. The data will illustrate how the Internet feeds a new culture of youth-built and youth-based activity which happens to meet both the needs and agenda of the white power movement. In this chapter, we will locate and define the qualities of that audience better known as the Net Generation and further identify important constructs of popular online culture. In fact, it is no coincidence that some of the same questions asked here mirror those that are constantly considered by the white power movement. Questions such as, Which forms of new media do teenagers and college students most visit online? What kinds of websites attract the most users? Why? What social issues speak to the browsing interests of today's young academic visitor? In a word, it's about identity. And understanding the personality of a typical Internet-user from the net generation can reveal more insight about those hate groups that are attempting to reach them.

Once the foundational, theoretical, and cultural elements of the white power movement in cyberspace have been examined, the next three chapters will present the fruits of their labor. Beginning with chapter 4, we will take a closer look at the 26 websites under review. For this, the white power movement itself will be presented in more exact terms relatable to these web communities of online hate. Like cyberspace itself, the network of the white power arena is vast. From the mainstays of white supremacist society, like the neo-Nazis and skinheads, to next generation racists, such as the Women for Aryan Unity, these homepages truly demonstrate the Internet's boundless potential to be a venue for all kinds of specialized interests.

An initial investigation of these homepages will look at the structural components of URLs like stormfront.org, jewwatch.com, and whitecivilrights.org. From there, research chapters 5 and 6 will delve deeper into the content of these sites by analyzing the packaging of educational and socially-geared messages within them. Through content and frame analysis, the research will peel back the presentation of white power "facts" and "information" and further dissect the underlying language of "friendly forums" in this social network to address two overlying questions. First, how has the white power movement adapted its cause into the information-providing/social networking culture of cyberspace? Second, how do these representative websites frame the white power message for the young-adult-user? These questions will guide a systematic breakdown of these 26 sites with closer attention paid to their mission statements, discussion boards, merchandise, and other measurable multi-media content.

Lastly, chapter 7 will come full circle to the other side of the democratic sphere where some community organizations have built their own websites for the purposes of monitoring hate group activity and promoting a new communication of tolerance. This chapter will highlight the ways that counteractive groups like the Anti-Defamation League (ADL), Southern Poverty Law Center, Simon Wiesenthal Center, and of course, local and federal law agencies are working to combat the white power movement's progression into the mainstream cyber culture. The private watchdog organizations, in particular, speak to the power of citizen groups on the web that use the same space to employ anti-hate speech measures and teaching tools as their weapons against racism. As Steele asserted in 1996, "The best remedy for hate speech is more speech. And the World Wide Web, which can be expanded infinitely, offers anyone who wishes to set up opposing viewpoints the opportunity to do so."[10] The civic potential of the web allows these groups to expose hate websites in order to confront the greater issue behind them – intolerance.

Finally, the larger audience will be addressed – that is, the primary audience of this text, students. As a generation practically born into the Internet, this group is perhaps at the greatest risk of falling into the trap of hate websites that are masked as pseudo-communities and research guides. In most cases, for instance, the college audience is twice and even three times removed from the generation that lived through the nightmare of the Holocaust. Does this make them more susceptible to websites that provide so-called proof that this event never actually occurred? Perhaps. The same target audience is also the generation that is rapidly moving away from traditional information sources like books whose paragraphs, pages and chapters are found in the greater context of libraries. Instead they are searching for answers to questions in online search engines, and finding them on homepages. Does this make them less likely to recognize certain fragmented information that is, in fact, well-crafted propaganda? In fact, it may, or it may not.

It could be that this audience will be *more* likely to recognize the falsities and pitfalls of the virtual world and even more aware of hate speech, because of the diversity of this net generation. While, of course, the coming chapters do not attempt to predict the future of an entire generation – only time will tell where the Internet age will lead them – one thing is certain. It is this net generation, and not the next, who will have to confront the growing current of hate speech on the Internet that is now spilling over into their popular culture. This young audience must learn to recognize all sides of the new democratic sphere in order to

---

[10] Shari Steele. "Taking a byte out of the first amendment." Human Rights: Journal of the Section of Individual Rights & Responsibilities, 23:2 (1996), 14-22.

safely navigate through the channels of cyberspace. In this in-
credibly complex age, that recognition process must begin by
first understanding what is and what is not racism.

Hate Speech, Radicals, and Codewords

So what is hate speech? As defined by McMasters (1999),
hate speech is "that which offends, threatens, or insults groups
based on race, color, religion, national origin, gender, sexual orientation, disability, or a number of other traits."[11] When thought
of as a functional component to the white power movement's
agenda, hate speech itself should be understood as something
more than the mere ranting and raving of a few fanatics. It is, in
fact, the technical craft of their trade which has steadily evolved
into a multifaceted stream of communication in white power society. Collectively, hate speech should be understood as the strategic employment of words, ideas, images, symbols, news items,
social issues, and even pop culture that have all become the
complex machinery of effective hate rhetoric – the kind that can
recruit a following. The Internet, with its own complex machinery of mass communication, has provided the white power
movement with a whole new arsenal of possibilities that like any
new threat must be investigated and properly understood.

But pursuing a contextual analysis of hate speech can quickly
lead the researcher into an unexpected maze of terminology,
heated politics and social debate. With every turn, there seems to
be a new trap door to avoid or fall through. When does the debate over affirmative action or immigration policy cross a line
into racist sentiment? What is the difference between Jewish and
Zionist? Does it matter with regard to anti-Semitism? If I am on
the far right or the far left of an issue, does that make me a "radical"? How far is too far...?

---

[11] Paul K. McMasters. "Must a Civil Society Be a Censored Society?"
Human Rights: Journal of the Section of Individual Rights & Responsibilities, 26:4 (1999), 1-7.

For American culture, the world's most diverse society, these questions are a part of life. This can be especially true when issues of race, religion, or sexual orientation enter into the public domain of the news media or popular culture where designations of political correctness are often validated, modified, or challenged. The Internet, however, is a much less filtered outlet. The infinite public square of discussion in cyberspace has stripped the boundaries of political correctness and free speech restraints, and in some ways, this can be a good thing. The anonymous nature of the web can provide a more candid and realistic view of American sentiment about race than we would typically receive in our other mass and personal communications. This is a necessary platform to have if we are to move forward as a multicultural society, but the gap between the virtual world and the actual one is wide when it comes to discussing matters of race, and many of those same questions and confusions remain.

In this research, it is important to provide a guide to approaching hate speech as an identifiable element in society and mass communication. The line that one crosses over from a politically heated debate into racist sentiment may be ambiguous, but it is not absent. This study contends that a strong divide *does* exist between hate speech and race debate. Whereas some would argue that racism exists at one end of the spectrum and healthy debate at the other, these two forms of communication are separated entirely by motive and emphasis. Those who engage in the debate over affirmative action, for instance, are most likely motivated by political, social, or economic issues, and as such, their contexts place emphasis on matters of jobs, equality, or fairness. Those who engage in hate speech *through* the affirmative action debate are only really motivated by the issue of identity, and this is seen in their words that place an emphasis on a people rather than the matter at hand. The most common example of this is the superiority/inferiority discourse that is present in most of these faux-political contexts.

When we separate debate and hate speech by their respective motives, public interest and racial identity, it becomes clear that there is not a solid spectrum of communication in all matters of race, but rather two separate lines with debate on one side, and hate on the other. In the United States, however, both forms of expression are protected under the same legal umbrella of the Constitution. As we will examine in the next chapter, the First Amendment does not discriminate between a spectrum of debate and the spectrum of hate on the Internet. However, in this contextual analysis, there is a functional value in noting not only the separation between the two forms of race communications, but more importantly, the way that white power movement websites borrow from the arguments and appearance of those closest in proximity to them on the farthest end of the debate side. In fact, that is their precise strategy.

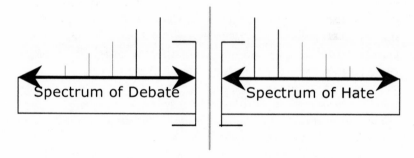

In this way, we see a complex dilemma in defining modern hate speech that looks and sounds just like the views of the far right or far left, depending on the issue. Using immigration as an example, at its core this debate is really about American citizenship, the economy, and national security with several perspectives emerging on either side of these arguments. Occasionally, the far right has infused the additional theme of nationalism into the case against immigration, which is not a form of hate speech, but which *can* be employed to bolster those that are such as hate groups that claim that Hispanic culture threatens white American society. The fact that concepts of *nationalism* and *culture war* exist on opposite plains of our working definitions of debate and hate speech is not as significant as the reality that they are only separated by a very thin line. The same narrow divide exists within movements on the far left as well, such as racial nationalist groups that express sweeping generalizations about white people or a white government, or the anti-religious movement that tends to vilify all of Judeo-Christian America. Each of these social-political expressions can easily fuel the larger fire of cultural intolerance building in American society regardless of whether or not that is their full intent.

In this study, some of the current contexts in which we will see white power movement websites exploiting that gray area between politics and radicalism include the issue of racial profiling in America, the president's nationality, gay marriage, the economic crisis, Wall Street scandals, political elections, and even family table issues like education and health care. Each of these recurring news cycles lends an element of race (some more than others) which the white power movement has keenly learned to utilize as ammunition on their websites. It becomes clear that the new voice of hate speech is now being spoken in the language of our politics, and not the actual racist belief system that lies beneath. So how do we recognize this belief system when we see it? This question brings us to our next contextual trap door, the code language of hate speech.

White power circles in the United States typically target the same minorities, most predominantly, Jews, African-Americans, Latin-Americans, Asian-Americans, and the gay and lesbian community. On occasion, their field of attack widens to include Native Americans, Indian Americans, Muslims, and certain Christian denominations. But, by and large, the typical white power websites and organizations concentrate their agendas on those which they often refer to on their websites as the "mud races."[12] However, because certain forms of hate speech in America are considered illegal, major hate groups like the National Alliance have learned to carefully direct their cause

---

[12] Harlan A. Loeb "Words Have Consequences: Reframing the Hate Speech Debate." Human Rights: Journal of the Section of Individual Rights & Responsibilities, 26:4 (1999), 11-18.

through more legitimate modes of communication. Enter the new lexicon of bigotry.

Code language in the white power arena is often very benign in appearance. Using some of the same terminologies common to political contexts, more messages of intolerance are being veiled beneath the cloak of socially accepted vernaculars. For example, the common expression "anti-American" seemingly denotes someone whose views are in opposition to the values of the United States and its people. In the online world of hate groups, however, anti-American refers to anyone that actively supports multicultural and progressive movements or that does not belong to the fabric of white society. The term is more frequently found within the context of radical right websites, meant to strike a cord with patriots that would naturally identify with any group of people claiming to be a part of "real" America. Of course, such language of exclusion is by design and intended to reach everyday white citizens who obviously would identify themselves as pro-American.

Like anti-Americanism, Zionism is another codeword often found in anti-Semitic corners of cyberspace. Zionism is commonly defined as the "movement for national revival and independence of the Jewish people in 'Eretz Yisrael'" (Israel by its biblical name).[13] Within the walls of white power websites, however, Zionism and Zionists mean but one thing – Jews. This intended conflation of meanings is a prime example of the white power movement hiding behind politically-acceptable language that does not directly implicate a people, but rather a movement identified with their ethnicity. In some circles, it's considered "fair play" to denigrate the Zionists as a people because there is a political context that exists between that word and the people it truly indicates. Many could therefore presume that the white power movement is staying safely within the boundaries of the spectrum of debate when they attack Zionists but not Jews, immigrants but not Hispanics, non-Europeans but not African-

---

[13] Susan H. Rolef (Ed.). Political Dictionary of the State of Israel. (Jerusalem, Israel: The Jerusalem Publishing House Ltd., 1993).

Americans, and anti-Americanism but not American multiculturalism – all code words for hate. As chapter 2 will later demonstrate, it is often, in fact, the *more* benign-sounding language of
encoded hate speech that has proven to be the most deadly.

Conclusion

Throughout history, powerful effects of propaganda – what
many media scholars commonly deem the "hypodermic needle"
of mass communication – have been crafted through encoded
racist sentiments and erroneous political causes in the media.
The popular Nazi newspapers and radio broadcasts of the 1930s
spoke directly to this point by consistently writing of a great Aryan heritage comprised of blonde hair and blue-eyed Germans,
while at the same time, reporting on Jewish fraud in the business
and academic fields. Encoded, these sentiments played out perfectly with a struggling German society to convey the idea that
Jews were not part of this great future Aryan Fatherland, but
rather were the people behind a deep conspiracy to control it. By
the late 1930s most German citizens did nothing when their Jewish neighbors were being taken from their houses and thrown
into cattle cars to destinations unknown, but suspected.

As the grandson of two Holocaust survivors of the Auschwitz
and Dachau concentration camps, my study of hate speech has
emanated from a desire to pursue the unanswered question of
how the fever of racist sentiment can so thoroughly sweep over a
civilized society as it did in 1930s Germany and other parts of
Europe.[14] Any research of the Holocaust will reveal that the systematic removal of Jews from society did not begin with the national march of anti-Semitic rallies through Nuremberg or the
riots of Cristalnacht, the Night of Broken Glass. It began in the

---

[14] Adam Klein's grandparents, Joe and Cecilie, were among the only
survivors of their families after the Holocaust. By chance, they were
reunited in Prague a few weeks after being liberated from separate concentration camps. They married shortly thereafter. Cecilie Klein. Sentenced to Live. (New York: Holocaust Library, 1989).

popular editorials of German newspapers like *Der Sturmer* and the political cartoons that depicted mainstream vilifications of the Jews. It began in the fringe media. These were the Nazi's greatest allies for turning the whole of German society against an entire people who had lived peacefully within their borders for centuries.

Understanding what constitutes hate speech today requires recognizing the same elements that were fundamental to the Nazi's formula: the courier, the message, and the medium. As we have already seen, the couriers of modern racism are a highly organized community of hate groups and individuals who are as multigenerational as they are media-savvy. While some may identify themselves as supremacists and others as separatists, their ideal American society is one and the same, white. The messages they deliver range across a wide spectrum of legally-protected hate speech, from outright and transparent bigotry to the evermore desirable gray area of race politics. To attain the type of mainstream following the Nazis achieved, today's couriers of hate are using a new medium that can reach millions in a matter of seconds, but most importantly, their number one target audience. That medium is the Internet, and its most common subscribers are the young adults of the net generation. We will soon see how the functions and formats of cyberspace accommodate both the needs of everyday young Americans, and at the same time, the agenda of white supremacist subculture. In this new dynamic, the latter will attempt to use the filters of education in cyberspace and social networks to interconnect their message of a white power uprising into the mainstream culture of the new media age.

1. Virtual Pleasure Island

In May, 2009, many Internet users read about the first high-profile case of a popular product of the web colliding with the elements of hate speech in cyberspace. The product is Facebook, the largest online community operating in cyberspace today and home to a staggering 20% of Internet users across the globe every month[15] Facebook has been an online social network since 2004, but over a decade later, it has also become a haven for a few unexpected residents of the online community – Holocaust denial groups. Among the sea of faces and profiles, mainly high school and college students, a new wave of memberships has surfaced dedicated to the cause of denying that the Holocaust ever occurred; that it was in fact a Jewish conspiracy.

Those who had heard this same rhetoric voiced before quickly recognized its subtext and responded, but not to the Holocaust deniers or to the White Pride groups that had also converged onto the mainstream website. Instead, attorneys like Brian Cuban decided to address Facebook directly, demanding that the Internet giant remove all those profiles that espoused any form of racist sentiment. In an open letter, Cuban wrote Facebook CEO, Mark Zuckerberg, to clarify that "the Holocaust denial movement is nothing more than a pretext to allow the preaching of hatred against Jews and to recruit other like-minded individuals to do the same."[16] Despite the fact that other hate watchdogs like the Simon Wiesenthal Center were suddenly alerting the popular site that it had become a recruiting ground for white power fanatics, Facebook executives ultimately decided not to remove the Holocaust denial groups, citing no clear violation had been made to their terms of service.

---

[15] Alexa Web Information. Retrieved on August 3, 2009, from http://alexa.com/siteinfo/facebook.com
[16] Douglas MacMillan. "Facebook's Holocaust Controversy." Retrieved August 3, 2009, from http://www.businessweek.com/technology/content/may2009/tc20090512_104433.htm

"Terms of Service." At the end of the day, these three words often constitute the only real law of the land in cyberspace. Regardless of whether the claim of hate speech was legitimate in this particular context, or the fact that Facebook is primarily a youth-based website, the news item that quickly ascended to national headlines disappeared just as fast having no legal ground to stand on. There simply was no existing precedent on which to base a case against hate speech on the Internet. The recent Facebook controversy, however, is only the tip of the iceberg in what is rapidly becoming a fiery litigious debate that addresses the real issue behind the news story. That is, the unguarded walls and "anything goes" atmosphere of the World Wide Web.

As many of us know, the Internet is not just a place for content to emerge and be shared among fellow users. Although most discussion and study today tends to focus on content alone, the Internet should also be recognized as a vast network of communities where people, in one sense or another, can actually go. When thought of in this manner, the young Internet-user enters into a virtual theme park every time they sign on. A fourteen-year-old, for instance, may visit any website they please, chat with new friends, join an online community, and perhaps take the relationship even further. The opportunities for interaction are endless and perhaps even thrilling for the younger generation who has yet to discover these things in their actual, real life form. But for all its thrills and virtual experience, the landscape of cyberspace is anything but a theme park. The difference here is that an actual park like Disneyworld, has cameras that monitor around every corner, safety measures on every ride, public security guards and police officers onsite, and of course, medical centers in case of an emergency. In most cases, these precautions are not just in place to please the park visitor, they are also the law.

So why are the most popular online communities for kids not treated with the same degree of protective measure and official oversight? Today, the answer to that question lies buried beneath the entangled infrastructure and legal framework of cyberspace. While traditional issues of free speech and media law go back to the earliest days of the American Revolution and the First

Amendment, respectively, their most current applications can be found in today's media outlets: books, newspapers, television programs, movies, radio, magazines, games and music. Here, we have seen issues like violence, obscenity, pornography, hate speech, and in particular, children's exposure to these elements of media debated in courts of law and official oversight agencies like the Federal Communications Commission (FCC). But those tangible pages of text, recordable images of television, and scripted scenes of movies each share qualities of media that are able to be safeguarded, monitored, and even prosecuted if need be in our measured system of free speech. That is because their media infrastructures, defined here as the composition of an industry and its products, are localized, i.e., books with identifiable authors and traceable origins.

Of course, no media system is ever fully free from laws and oversight, otherwise anyone with a platform could falsely cry fire in a crowded theatre, steal copyrighted material, libel a private citizen, publish photos of child pornography, or call for the killing of an entire race of people. In the traditional mediums of American media, the legal groundwork for such cases has already been laid through issues like ownership, access, trademarks, but most of all, content as it relates to free speech in the public sector. Even when these localized media go too far, such rare incidences are easily isolated, their questionable content debated on established ground, and if necessary, consequences delivered to the appropriate accountable inscriber. But in cyberspace, none of these essential constructs exist. In fact, the very infrastructure of the web is so complex that the potential for regulating any part of it is nearly impossible.

While it would seem that the same laws which apply to the actual world should likewise apply to the virtual one, van Dijk (2005) reminds us that "existing legislation depends on clearly demonstrable, localizable and liable legal persons and ownership titles."[17] On the Internet, clear lines of jurisdiction have been

---

[17] Jan van Dijk. The Network Society: Social Aspects of New Media. (Thousand Oaks, CA: Sage Publications, Second Edition, 2005).

replaced by networks connecting to other networks worldwide, and often the Internet user is only as identifiable as their screen name allows. It soon becomes apparent that the World Wide Web is far too open-ended and undefined in terms of its access points, owners, and jurisdiction to approach the issue of "dangerous speech" with any real authority or consequence. The result of these unparalleled freedoms is also apparent.

For popular social networks like Facebook, YouTube, and Twitter, there are currently no laws in place that force these, or any other website for that matter, to monitor and record their chat rooms and content made available to children, and no online agency to report to in the event that something does go wrong. Legally, the young Internet user becomes an ideal target in this world, in part because of their impressionable minds, but also because the community itself goes virtually unchecked by any true authority and entrance at the gate is free.

Where is Cyberspace?

If you imagine yourself as a regulator of the media or perhaps an investigator of a cyber crime, or simply a parent concerned over their child's online activities, the path to discovery begins at the click of the Internet icon on your desktop. However, once you enter that digital doorway you might as well be stepping off a ledge into space itself. The greatest challenge in monitoring, regulating, or simply defining the Internet is first pinpointing its actual location. But unlike the printing presses that generate books and newspapers, or radio towers that transmit music and commercials, the locality of cyberspace is in no way central to one point. As Einzinger explains:

> On the Internet, central nodes, where you could effectively monitor the data flow, just don't exist. At the point of origin, content is split into many small data pockets that seek their way through networks on their own and are reassembled at the point of destination. There are many, many routes to get from "A to B" on the Internet. Remember: the Internet con-

sists of a myriad of IP networks and Internet service providers can only see and monitor their own small part.[18]

Adding to the complexity of information flow is the reality that Internet Service Providers are centered all over the world, from Silicon Valley to Singapore, where they launch private websites that quickly become interlinked to other sites with different web hosts, perhaps even operating from other countries. In this way, the Internet is easily the most anonymous, decentralized, and hence, non-traceable form of media that the world has ever seen.

Many have cited the decentralization of cyberspace as one of the key factors in its global success and public embrace as a democratic sphere of communication. This argument is also rooted in the fact that the World Wide Web provides nearly anyone with an inexpensive platform for instantly reaching a potential audience of millions. For the countless social movements and public causes that function around the globe, this open access means they no longer need a podium and a microphone to reach the most immediate masses. In fact, they don't even need a face – they simply require Internet access. In *Reno v. ACLU,* the U.S. Supreme Court finally weighed in on the "vast democratic forums of the Internet" in their most definitive function:

> Through the use of chat rooms, any person with a phone line can become a town crier with a voice that resonates farther than it could from any soapbox. Through the use of the Web pages, mail exploders, and newsgroups, the same individual can become a pamphleteer…"[T]he content on the Internet is as diverse as human thought."[19]

---

[18] Kurt Einzinger. "Media Regulation on the Internet." In "Hate Speech on the Internet." Retrieved August 1, 2009, from http://www.osce.org/publications/rfm/2004/12/ 12239_94_en.pdf, 142-149.

[19] Seth F. Kreimer. "Technologies of Protest: Insurgent Social Movements and the First Amendment in the Era of the Internet." University of Pennsylvania Law Review, 150:1 (2001), 119-125.

Perhaps the diversity of that human thought can best be attributed to a network that is not localized, but rather decentralized, global, and also very much anonymous. While the anonymity of cyberspace can afford certain social movements a greater freedom to express their beliefs, such as in those countries that outlaw public debate in a state-run press system, there are other beneficiaries of this online obscurity whose motives are not as altruistic.

The great vastness and anonymity of the Internet has provided an ideal space for white supremacists and other anti-social movements to reemerge in a mainstream medium that is far less transparent than a sidewalk rally or a television news interview. In "Anonymity, Democracy and Cyberspace" Akdeniz (2002) posits that, "As a concept anonymity is closely related to free speech and privacy. Internet technology allows for anonymous communications and this can be used for several purposes, including those that are socially useful and those that are criminal."[20] For the white power movement, the anonymous and decentralized infrastructure of the Internet means that they, too, are no longer localized. Like all social movements, hate groups which had never before had an audience larger than their most immediate regions can instantly transmit their message all over the world, while at the same time, remain safely hidden on the web.

In effect, the global connection has instantly turned the basement subculture of hate groups like the Hammerskin Nation into an organized and international movement. Incidentally, the Hammerskin homepage currently features flags that represent chapters from all corners of the world. As a function of cyberspace, sites like these are now able to capitalize on their new-found global access through the power of links. The Creativity Alliance website, for instance, provides connections to its sister sites in Australia, Germany, Croatia, and Slovakia, while Storm-front.org, the largest international hate website, provides links to

---

[20] Yaman Akdeniz. "Anonymity, Democracy, and Cyberspace." Social Research, 69:1 (2002), 224.

its chapters in Italy, Spain, the United Kingdom, Canada, France, Russia, South Africa and nine other countries within this global network. In any number of languages, this trend exemplifies the medium of the Internet in which anyone can extend a centralized social movement into another country, thus connecting once fragmented communities and causes beyond borders. In Stormfront en Francais, a new forum about Jewish people reads, "Notre veritable ENNEMI." Translation: Our true ENEMY.[21]

In addition to expansion, the Internet has also provided the white power movement with the opportunity to exploit another legal dilemma of the web infrastructure. That is the regulation of a global media market where lines of jurisdiction are as vague as they are nearly untraceable. Perhaps more than any other element of cyberspace, the jurisdiction of intellectual property across international borders has been given the greatest amount of global legal attention to date. Typically these nonbinding resolutions have centered on issues of copyrights, trademarks, and patents. Regardless of legal zone, Steele (1996) asserts that "there are some problems with applying currently existing laws to cyberspace. Unlike in the physical world, there is no physical location where these communications take place, making it difficult to determine where violations of law should be prosecuted."[22] As many legislators and law enforcement officials quickly discovered, the mere act of locating criminal conduct or content on the web does not necessarily pinpoint the actual location of its inscriber. Further, if that inscriber is beyond the physical limitations of the local authority, who is to say which agency, national or international, would even enforce it? This is great news for those wishing to test the laws of hate speech in the new medium. It also leads us to another factor of even greater consequence for

---

[21] Stormfront En Français. Retrieved October 25, 2007, from http://www.stormfront.org/forum/forumdisplay.php/stormfront-en-fran-ais-69.html

[22] Shari Steele. "Taking a byte out of the first amendment." Human Rights: Journal of the Section of individual Rights & Responsibilities, 23:2 (1996), 14-22.

the white power movement: In cyberspace, locality is not just an issue of jurisdiction – it's a matter of culture.

Because the Internet knows no national boundaries, the chances of being exposed to the cultures of other societies are far greater than in any other medium. However, with this constant influx and fusing of international culture – the great "global village" that Marshall McLuhan (1964) once predicted[23] – the world community is inevitably exposed to contrasting definitions of ethics, values, and legalities. A common example of this is the issue of child pornography. In the United States, laws *and* culture deem that a child under the age of 17 is a minor and it is considered illegal and immoral to produce pornographic material featuring minors in any platform of society including the Internet. Other countries, however, have different standards as to what age divides child from adult and what constitutes illegal pornography. In much the same way, the culture dilemma has also challenged the issue of hate speech in cyberspace.

In Einzinger's 2002 analysis of *Media Regulation on the Internet*, he notes that "in some Central European countries there is strict legislation against right wing extremism (neo-Nazism), but this is absent from most other countries. Therefore there are some neo-Nazi sites on the Web which cannot be removed because their servers are located in countries where there are no legal grounds for their removal" (p. 143). One such nation that fits this bill as a prime location for extremists to flourish within its wide open servers: the United States. While America's legal system does include laws aimed at criminalizing certain forms of hate speech, such legislation is narrowly defined and rarely tried in a court of law. This makes the web hosts that operate on American soil the new safe houses for white power fanatics that would otherwise be prosecuted in nations that outlaw these forms of hate speech –

---

[23] Marshall McLuhan. Understanding media: The extensions of man. (Cambridge, MA: MIT Press, 1964).

including Holocaust denial – such as Germany, Austria, France, Poland, Israel, Spain, and the Czech Republic.[24]

For some, the intercultural environment of cyberspace simply delivers an awesome vehicle for arriving at unlimited information and diversity. For others, it becomes a virtual "pleasure island" for uninhibited racists to express their resentments toward diversity itself, while at the same time, expanding their own communities worldwide. Even as new cases arise in the public domain, such as the Facebook controversy, regulating the borders of cyberspace along the same lines of all other media jurisdictions still leaves one all important entity unaddressed.

Who is Accountable?

The question of accountability in cyberspace is almost as complex as the concept of locality. In fact, they are practically one and the same, but with regard to the legal contexts of hate speech the issue of a website's locality only establishes the scene of the crime while the underlying matter of accountability aims to determine the criminal party. Once again, the Internet's own infrastructure presents a challenge to the task of determining accountability in terms of a website's content. For as long as mass communication has been an industry, the process of arriving at fault in civil cases of the media have usually rested on the shoulders of whichever individual, company, or organization was responsible for delivering that media product into the public domain. Sometimes there can be more than one offender. In matters of libel in an authored work, for instance, both the writer and publisher can be held accountable for the fraudulent content of a book if it is deemed damaging to the plaintiff. A more applicable example might be if a magazine article advocates for violent action against illegal Hispanic immigrants, then the journal's

---

[24] Michael J. Bazyler. Holocaust Denial Laws and Other Legislation Criminalizing Promotion of Nazism. Retrieved August, 1, 2009, from http://www1.yadvashem.org/about_yad/departments/ audio/Bazyler.pdf (2006)

publisher would likely be found responsible for propagating the illegal form of hate speech. In many ways, publishers of traditional media outlets like these are the industry's self-regulating boundary between an author whose work goes too far and the public domain that might have received it. On the Internet, however, no such boundary exists because anyone can be a publisher.

If thought of as a giant bookstore where both products and ideas are sold, the Internet has no discretion over what items will stock its shelves. All one needs in this day and age to publish an idea or ignite a cause is a website and an Internet Service Provider (ISP) to disseminate that content. Most of the time ISPs are like storage facilities, unaware of the content they host. And without incentive to do so, why would they? For ISPs that specialize in web hosting, there are no legal ramifications that would deem them a "publisher" should one of their websites or blogs publish something illegal. According to Shyles (2003), "There has been dispute over whether ISP's are publishers or distributors. This classification is important because it is often difficult to track down the originator of a defamatory statement on the Internet."[25] For the white supremacy website, this is both good and bad news. On one hand, it allows any hate-based organization ease with which to post any matter of content on the web, because as Shyles further explains, it is in the best interest of an ISP to "avoid exercising any kind of editorial control or parental screening in order to avoid liability as publishers." On the other hand, as publishers of the website, the hate group inscriber can be held liable for any practiced form of speech that is not protected by the First Amendment, i.e. libel, slander (via audio podcasts), or more relevant to these purposes, speech that is deemed "threatening or harassing."

But the concept of the 'online publisher' has become even more lost in cyberspace as the infrastructure of the Internet has

---

[25] Leonard Shyles. Deciphering Cyberspace: Making the Most of Digital Communication Technology. (Thousand Oaks, CA: Sage Publications, 2003), 343.

become even more democratic. What was once understood as a media outlet comprised of websites that were essentially book-ended by their homepages and last pages, the Internet has now become a multidimensional channel of communicative plat-forms. From video-sharing to online radio, commercial journal-ism to civic reporting, social networks to opinion-driven blogs; the concept of the Internet publisher encompasses all functions of the converging media space. And the white power movement makes use of all of them on its websites and can continue to do so as long as the question of web responsibility remains unclear. This lack of clarity is reflected in specific cases that address sev-eral intangibles of online content. Questions like, does a news base like CNN.com bear equal responsibility over the comments of the readers that follow its news articles? Or, more suited to our purposes is the question of whether an anti-Semitic website can be held accountable if one of its members posts a forum calling for the killing of Jews. What if they or one of the other members acts on the call?

Perhaps one the greatest challenges to monitoring and in some cases preventing the published agenda of hate groups on the Internet is designating the actual identity of the publisher behind the privacy of their screen name. As we have discussed, anonymity in cyberspace is one of the medium's most liberating features affording all Internet users a blanket of security in com-munications that the real world does not. But anonymity for the racist minds of society can mean something else entirely. In their exploration of the psychological uses of the Internet, Magdoff and Rubin (2003) remind us that "on the Net you need not nec-essarily be who you were when you turned on the com-puter...you may switch gender, shave years off your age."[26] In this sense, the Internet provides its users more than just anonym-ity; it allows them to become a different version of themselves all

---

[26] JoAnn Magdoff and Jeffrey B. Rubin. "Social and Psychological Uses of the Internet." In Leonard Shyles' (ed.) Deciphering Cyberspace: Making the Most of Digital Communication Technology. (Thousand Oaks, CA: Sage Publications, 2003) 201-216.

together. This is significant because it has led to a much freer form of indulgence on the Internet regarding issues which are normally considered taboos of external society, but which have flourished in the secret confines of cyberspace. In this world, Internet users with fictitious names can view any obscene material from any country, visit a chat room to rendezvous with a complete stranger, or even join a community that promotes ideas like white supremacy and racial war. Of course, most everyday citizens are not interested in these offerings, but those few who are have benefited greatly from the web culture of anonymity and legal loopholes of unaccountability.

In time, the questions of online accountability will be addressed, though most likely on the grounds of something more mainstream such as information-sharing, i.e., whether a public encyclopedia like Wikipedia is responsible for cases of libel or copyright infringement on its shared information space. Or perhaps a clearer definition of accountability will emerge out of one of the many convergent media centers, such as whether a site like YouTube is liable if a defamatory video is broadcasted within its broad domain. In the mean time, this subject is still quite open to interpretation. As for the inscribers of hate speech, the umbrella of cyberspace continues to provide enough cover for hate websites, such as those examined in this study, to develop comfortably within its broad legal limits.

One of the primary reasons for the uninhibited development of hate speech in the American sector of cyberspace has to do with the nature of one of the only pieces of existing Internet legislation, the Child Online Protection Act (COPA), passed by Congress in its 1998 budget bill. With regard to content, COPA sought to "narrow the scope of law" regarding harmful online material for kids.[27] The problem with COPA, aside from the free speech debate that surrounds it, is that this measure is aimed specifically at protecting children from obscene content or sexual

---

[27] Jan Samoriski. Issues in Cyberspace: Communication, Technology, Law, and Society on the Internet Frontier. (Boston, MA: Allyn and Bacon, 2002) 286.

contact from an online stranger. While the bill certainly looks after the interests and well-being of the young Internet generation, it has also left the door to the white power community wide open for minors to enter, interact, and join. Like COPA, the FCC has also placed a much greater emphasis on issues of obscenity and sexual content in the media than on communicated acts of violence which are treated as a far lesser offense. The irony of these examples is that racial hate speech is much more mainstreamed and accessible these days on the World Wide Web than sites dedicated to sexual content, many of which are increasingly preceded by a disclaimer aimed at restricting the entry of minors. Hate websites, on the other hand, have no such warnings.

Finally, there is one more all important element of online hate speech that keeps its many inscribers out of the courts and behind their monitors spewing out their rant of racial bigotry. That element is hate speech itself, by its legal classification, which most U.S. courts have defined along the narrowest of interpretations so as to protect the integrity and strength of American free speech. But in practical terms, the narrow space that legally defines what constitutes actual hate speech has left a great deal of breathing room for the white power movement to communicate its own warped values and underlying intentions, online.

The Legal Landscape of Hate Speech

Hate speech has been called "the Pandora's box in American legal debates."[28] While unpopular speech in the United States is constitutionally-protected in the marketplace of ideas, a few state courts have introduced exceptions to certain forms of speech where language has been used to promote or incite violence against a person or group of people. Certainly free speech, popular or not, is the essential component and centerpiece to any

---

[28] Paul J. Becker, Bryan Byers, and Arthur Jipson. "The Contentious American Debate: The First Amendment and Internet-based Hate Speech." International Review of Law Computers, 14:1 (2000) 33-41.

working democracy. Even with regard to this subject matter, McMaster's (1999) aptly reminds us that, "Hate speech uncovers the haters." If for no other reason than to protect the First Amendment in cyberspace, where hate is rampant, is that it locates, tracks, exposes, and informs us about the racist elements of our society. However, the steady spikes in racial violence over the years stemming from fanatic individuals of mainly white power ideals have led a handful of courts across the country to tighten their definitions of what constitutes "free speech" to exclude certain forms of hateful rhetoric.

In *Chaplinsky vs. New Hampshire*, the court ruled that "fighting words" – those that "(1) 'by their very utterance inflict injury' and (2) 'tend to incite an immediate breach of the peace'" are in fact, unlawful.[29] Over the last century other cases have rendered decisions that added more terminologies like "clear and present danger," "incitement to…imminent lawless action," and the "heckler's veto" to the growing litany of legislation.[30] In the *Beauharnais vs. Illinois* case, it was even declared illegal to "advertise, publish, present or exhibit…the citizen of any race, color, creed or religion to contempt, derision, or obloquy." While these various state decisions have never managed to successfully challenge the Supreme Court's overriding view of the First Amendment, which still maintains the broadest definition, they have represented the more local response to racism. This response is perhaps indicative of the nearly one-third of Americans who think it is "a good idea to ban hate speech" according to a 2008 Rasmussen poll. One year later (and just two weeks after the Holocaust museum shooting), another poll conducted by the same group found that 50% of Americans now "believe hate is

---

[29] Dale Herbeck. "Chaplinsky v. New Hampshire." In Richard Parker's (ed.) Free Speech on Trial: Communication Perspectives on Landmark Supreme Court Decisions. (Tuscaloosa, AL: University of Alabama Press, 2003) 85–99.

[30] Paul K. McMasters. "Must a Civil Society Be a Censored Society?" Human Rights: Journal of the Section of Individual Rights & Responsibilities, 26:4 (1999).

growing in America" while 44% feel that "extreme political rhetoric on the radio, television and the Internet lead to increased hate in America."[31]

As students of media, mass communications, and information these polls and the sorted legislation of local courts should tell us two things about this issue. First, that the grassroots debate surrounding hate speech is very much divided across the country, and it is fair to assume that this can largely be attributed to varied understandings of what actually constitutes hate speech, legal or not. Second, that this issue is not just about public or legal views on racism, but rather it concerns language. Many of the attempts to pinpoint a working legal definition of hate speech have sought to do so by drawing a line of illegality at that point where the rhetoric promotes violent action – "fighting words" or "clear and present danger." However, as we know language itself is so much more complex and capable than these exacting terms would suggest.

The mere expulsion of "fighting words" from the public domain does not necessarily condemn the voices of anti-Semitism or racism by itself nor has it stopped them from inciting actual harm to others. In fact, most white supremacy groups have adapted with these times by employing language that sells their cause while carefully *not* publishing words that spell out violence. One of the primary goals of this research aimed to look at ways that the white power movement's online message manages to suggest actions without articulating a direct form of the illegal diction listed above. As later chapters will show, there are a number of ways to advocate for aggressive action through subtext and suggestion. Further, in many cases, the examples in this study clearly did cross the line of illegality into expressions of racial violence and action.

While it is important to begin any investigation of hate speech with a legal consideration of this complex issue, a greater

---

[31] 50% Say Hate Is Growing in America. Retrieved on July 1, 2009, from http://www.rasmussenreports.com/public_content/lifestyle/general_lifestyle/june_2009/50_say_hate_is_growing_in_america

significance lies in understanding the culture of its domain on the Internet. That culture is the net generation of kids, teenagers and college students who use the Internet as a tool for research and a social network among friends. Returning to the practical matter of online hate speech, the real concern for most authorities, legal or public, is the amplified exposure of young adults to outright racism and hate within the mainstream platform of cyberspace. It is therefore no wonder that some of the more recent issues emerging about hate speech on the Internet center on one of the most protected environments *for* children, education.

In many schools across the United States, local boards of education have begun to institute "intolerance filters" onto computers in attempt to seal off potential gateways to harmful material for aspiring minds. These same filters that seek out websites dedicated to racism have already become the public knowledge of many hate groups who have responded by providing their own counter measures, such as instructional forums titled, "how to bypass filters at work or school" and "does your school block this site?"[32] Other districts have taken it upon their own authority to ban access to the popular video-sharing website YouTube on school grounds. The unfiltered media site is one of the most frequented among the net generation, but as many teachers and local district leaders have observed, it is also rapidly becoming a viral breeding ground for films that express "anti-Semitism and misogyny and homophobia."[33] These widely accessible hate-films are far from isolated incidents. Even among themselves, the capacity of these websites allows other users to generate hundreds of thousands of comments for a single posting, and so racist rhetoric stemming from one hate-film tends to grow and grow.

---

[32] Stormfront.org (2009). Does your school block this site? Retrieved on August 4, 2009, from
http://www.stormfront.org/forum/sitemap/index.php/t-269822.html
[33] Will Doig. "Homophobosphere." The Advocate, 1002. Retrieved on August 1, 2009, from http://www.advocate.com/
issue_story_ektid51690.asp (2008)

This trend is certainly not what Marshall McLuhan had in mind when he once wrote of a global village.

Returning to the earlier case of Facebook and the Holocaust denial groups, a similar theme is present in this news story of the injection of hateful information into a youth-driven medium. The keyword here is information. In this instance, Holocaust denial groups and a few members directly affiliated with anti-Semitic organizations are using the community of Facebook to "inform" other inscribers about an alternate "history." A supposed history of the Holocaust that never was, and an invented conspiracy that was perpetrated by the Jews.

Like Facebook, other mainstream websites have also become the unwitting facilitators of the white power movement as it seeks to benefit from their open infrastructures, in particular sites that provide paths to information or research. Websites like Amazon and Google will play a starring role in the next chapter that moves toward a new theoretical understanding of the process by which cyber hate is transforming into online information. However, for now it is sufficient to say that the unregulated environment of cyberspace has posed a real challenge for educators and information specialists alike that utilize the web to teach the next generation. It seems that just as they are introducing young minds to new technologies and democratic modes of communication, hate groups are using those same tools for their own nefarious purposes in their race to win over the digital generation. And the underlying question remains, what is to stop them?

There are currently no legal grounds upon which to stop a neo-Nazi group from entering into a public network community like Facebook, MySpace, or Disney for that matter, nor is there a precedent that would aptly challenge the kinds of hate speech that are infiltrating the search engine universe of information gatherers everyday. Today, it is important to begin to recognize that these vulnerabilities exist in cyberspace, not for the sake of challenging the First Amendment, but rather to understand exactly how it is that this space operates to the benefit and opportunism of those who would seek to exploit its unique media framework.

Conclusion

In many ways, the exceptional trait of cyberspace, its unlimited public space for free expression, is also its Achilles heel. The fact that there is no velvet rope to keep underage users from entering certain domains is matched by the reality that there is also no detectors that prohibit hate groups from entering that same space. Culture has also played a large role in developing the infrastructure of cyberspace into a center that embraces the informal, anything goes attitude of a younger generation. There are also very few gatekeepers in this new medium whereas the traditional media like television and radio are supported and in many ways protected by an established network of keepers that funnel through the desirable content and weed out the rest. With the exception of commercial pay-to-enter websites, the territory is also wide open and available to anyone wishing to plot their own website, as Internet space is very cheap real estate.

The legal landscape of cyberspace presents something of a paradox. In one respect, the transparent infrastructure of the Internet provides an open window into communities of concern for law enforcement agencies; terrorist cells, radical political groups, the white power movement. For each of these extremist organizations with a website, there is no doubt a team of officials monitoring it closely, not to mention the watchful eyes of numerous civil rights groups. However, in another respect, this remarkable looking glass is nothing more than an illusion. What one sees on the screen before them is a website created in one place but hosted in another. Its location is ambiguous at best in this vast digital universe, and its inscribers – perhaps present in published form – are still quite invisible. The privacy of the Internet is secured in passwords, screen names, avatars, and a decentralized framework that presents a liberating environment for many of its users. For others, like parents, teachers, and law enforcement, its anonymity poses a series of dangerous prospects.

The answer to addressing the perils of cyberspace, however, is not as complex as it may seem. While there are some who advocate strongly for more regulations on the web, reducing free speech in any venue is seldom the solution. The public square of the World Wide Web thrives only because it is part of an open democratic network. Some American civil rights groups have also argued for more restrictions on hate speech itself by adopting the same measures as many European countries have in prohibiting the propagation, publishing, or broadcasting of racist sentiments. But these measures have actually done very little to abate the real problem of racial intolerance and widespread anti-Semitism in Europe. In the end, the greater issue behind hate speech is still active in societies both here and abroad. The real answer then is education. Rather than restricting the Internet with regulations and filters, or silencing hate speech in the public domain, each of which could later inhibit our own freedoms, the net generation must become informed about the existence of these racist elements in actual society and alerted to their broadening agendas in cyberspace. Through *more* speech, not less, an open dialogue about online hate today can begin to lift the veil of anonymity from white power groups in cyberspace and uncover the actual movement behind these communities.

2. Hate Speech in the Information Age

When the *Protocols of the Elders of Zion* hit bookstands in Russia, its pages circulated swiftly through the streets and halls of society. Within a few years, the book rose in readership and distinction across much of Western Europe where it was being heralded in major newspapers such as the *Times* of London and *Morning Post*. Even more significant than the *Protocols'* popularity on bookshelves was its circulation among the leading libraries of Paris, Berlin, Tokyo, and New York where it was not only treated as a piece of literature, but as an informational artifact come to light. In this recently discovered book lay the proof of a Jewish conspiracy to take over the world, unearthed and exposed for all to read. It was all there in black and white and narrated form, inscribed from the hands of Jewish elders who had attended a secret meeting of the Zionist Congress where this plot had been sewn and recorded. That plot: "To destroy empires and annihilate peoples, the Jews [will] hatch revolutions."[34]

There was only one problem with this text, aside from the arduous task of translating its millions of copies around the world in Russian, English, Arabic, and every European language. The *Protocols of the Elders of Zion* was a fake. A complete forgery aimed at linking the evils of democracy and liberalism with an already familiar enemy, the Jews, the *Protocols* put into false words what a few anti-Semites had dreamed up using plagiarized works that were not even about the Jews. The *Protocols* was eventually proven a forgery when its contents were traced almost verbatim to an obscure French text that had been written over thirty years prior. However, the actual revelation of this propaganda is not as significant as the sheer complexity of its method, achieved through the crafting of literature, manipulation of print indus-

---

[34] Binjamin W. Segel (1995). A Lie and a Libel: The History of the Protocols of the Elders of Zion. (Lincoln, NE: University of Nebraska Press, 1995) 56.

tries, archiving of books, and exploitation of libraries, newspapers, and scholars. Even more astounding than this sophisticated heist of the media is the time in which it occurred – at the end of the 1800s.

The Protocols of the Elders of Zion is one of the earliest examples of racial intolerance disguised in the form of a "discovered" piece of information. Written in 1897 at the instruction of members of the Russian secret police who were intent on quelling the Czar's interest in democracy and modernism, the *Protocols* set out to present the "institutions of liberalism" as the very tools by which Jews were going to bring down world civilizations, *like* Russia. According to Segel (1995), liberal ideas like "equality of all citizens before the law, freedom of conscience and religion, freedom of the press, compulsory education, universal suffrage [and] constitutional government" were beginning to threaten the autocracy in Russia at the turn of the century when the staged discovery of the *Protocols* helped to subdue that movement by casting its principles as the ploy of a Jewish conspiracy (p. 57). So powerful is this method of hate speech when done effectively that it can remain active in the annals of bigoted conspiracy theorists even after its refutation, and later reemerge in the public domain as forgotten fact with renewed vigor. Similar examples of this phenomenon include the select misinterpretation of Charles Darwin's *Theory of Evolution*, used as "genuine" proof that black men were somehow less evolved than whites, or the infamous "blood libel" that for centuries maintained that Jews were using the blood of Christian children for their rituals. Each of these lingering examples managed to sustain their forged legitimacy because they were born in the trusted circles of scholarship of their time, science and the church, respectively.

Such was also the case with the *Protocols*, which was not only supported by the likes of a young Winston Churchill, but also propagated regularly by American auto tycoon Henry Ford in his *Dearborn Independent* that ran articles like, "The International

Jew, The World's Problem."[35] Ultimately the counterfeit Zionist document would become a major influence on Adolf Hitler's scholastic beginnings as referenced in his book *Mein Kampf* and the devastating anti-Semitic campaign to follow. Sixty years after the Holocaust, *The Protocols of the Elders of Zion* is still being sold in bookstores around the globe from the Far East to the Middle East and in countless Western cities like Paris, Venice, Mexico City, San Diego and New Orleans.[36]

The success of this, one of the oldest pieces of mediated propaganda in modern history, can only be understood by examining the elements, practices, and theories behind an unlikely pairing in the field of mass communications: information and hate speech. When put together, the communicative compound of racist-propaganda can prove even more damaging and deadly than outright bigotry which is often recognized as such and quickly disregarded by most everyday citizens. Information-based propaganda, however, does not even need to find expression beneath the radar of civil society. In fact, the actual intent of this form of hate speech is to be discovered and validated on an intellectual ground, particularly by way of the media where, within reputable outlets like newspapers, books, and journals, racist ideas can be transformed into public knowledge.

The practice of sowing hateful bigotry into legitimate sources of information became something of a sinister art form in the 20th Century when mass media itself became a penetrating force in the daily lives of all citizens, and radical movements learned to wield that power of mass communication. Studies in propaganda developed into serious investigations in the fields of psychology, political science, and communication after World War II when humanity saw the full extent of media's power exemplified by the Nazi's masterful dissemination of Jewish-hate across all of Ger-

---

[35] Jeffrey Herf. The Jewish Enemy: Nazi Propaganda During World War II and the Holocaust. (Cambridge, MA: The Belknap Press of Harvard University press, 2006) 81.
[36] Will Eisner. The Plot: The Secret Story of The Protocols of the Elders of Zion. (New York: W.W. Norton & Company, 2005).

many, Poland, and Czechoslovakia. From the early work of centers like the U.S. Institute for Propaganda Analysis[37] (1937-1942)
to more contemporary studies by scholars like Jowett and
O'Donnell[38] (2005) and Herman and Chomsky[39] (2002), people
have long sought to understand how sophisticated, educated societies can become conditioned, and even brainwashed, by the
everyday devices of mass communication. In the most extreme
cases, we have seen these same devices used as the delivery systems for broadcasting nationwide genocides (Bosnia 1992-1995,
Rwanda 1994, Darfur 2003 to present day). But what are these
devices? And how does hateful propaganda funnel into the ordi-
nary lives of everyday people?

Today, the answers to both those questions lie in the overwhelming diffusion of informational objects that constantly oc-
cupy the spaces of our lives. From cell phones to personal digital
assistants (PDAs), cable TVs to portable DVDs, electronic billboards to personal computers, it seems that screens of all functions and sizes have oversaturated our worlds. Lester and
Koehler, Jr. (2003) assert that "one result of this proliferation is
an increased dependency on these information devices to structure daily life."[40] For the able propagandist, the utmost important concepts in that sentiment are "dependency" and "structure." To understand where a society's dependencies lie and how
the daily life is structured is to hold the keys to unlocking and
forming public opinion. In many ways, propagandists are no dif-

---

[37] Karen S. Johnson-Cartee and Gary Copeland. Strategic Political
Communication: Rethinking Social Influence, Persuasion, and Propaganda. (Lanham, MD: Rowman & Littlefield Publishers, 2003) 167.
[38] Garth S. Jowett and Victoria O'Donnell. Readings in Propaganda
and Persuasion: New and Classic Essays (Thousand Oaks, California:
SAGE Publications, 2005).
[39] Edward Herman and Noam Chomsky. Manufacturing Consent: The
Political Economy of the Mass Media. (New York: Pantheon Books, a
division of Random House, Inc., 2002).
[40] June Lester and Wallace C. Koehler, Jr. Fundamentals of Information Studies: Understanding Information and Its Environment. (New
York: Neal-Schuman Publishers, Inc., 2003)

ferent than advertisers or public relations specialists. They each strive to ascertain the interests of a target audience, as well as the entrance points of media within that community, and the types of communication that will appeal to the public's opinion. The main difference is that racial propagandists are not selling any real products or legitimate ideas, but rather their own fabricated reality built upon what they purport to be true, as well as what they craftily choose to omit. The "fine art of propaganda," as Lee and Lee called it, is a complex stratagem of cleverly formu-lated meanings that begin with the nature of the message, i.e., religious, cultural, political, or as this research submits the most effective, informational.

Just as the Russian secret police used the media structure of the early 20th Century to introduce the *Protocols* into that informa-tion-dependent society, so too does today's white power move-ment employ the central knowledge-providing tool of the 21st Century. That tool of course is the Internet, through which cen-ters for scientific research, literature, history, politics, and current events – all areas which have been exploited by propagandists in the past – have converged onto one central space, making it con-venient for today's messengers of hate to "inform" the next gen-eration. However, before examining the practices of modern day racial propagandists, we must understand how the fusion of hate speech and information have evolved together, and often rein-vented itself over time, to arrive at this point. We begin with the most notorious example of this particular venomous strand of propaganda – the Nazi model.

"The Ministry of Public Enlightenment"

By nature, media and information speaks to the cultural trends of a people the same way that laws often reflect the cli-mate of a government. Under a microscope of time, one can look to the media of a generation to discover tangible indicators of a society that listened to its broadcasts, purchased its music, and read its newspapers. In the 1930s, the very same German media that ushered in the latest films and music from around the world was also subtly ushering in the winds of intolerance, followed by a national fervor of anti-Semitism through blatant media bias, and not-so-blatant propaganda. Most of the print and film of the time were produced by the rapidly building Nazi party, and some of it was also the product of everyday citizen-fanatics. Newspapers like *Der Stürmer,* anti-Semitic cartoons and billboards, even children's books like *The Poison Mushroom* were not simply forms of cultural expression, but the quiet pulse of a nation beating toward new themes of blame and intolerance of the Jews.[41] The more one examines the publishers, producers and the owners of such anti-Semitic media, literature, and informational sources, the more they begin to discover the means by which the voices of a few translated into the voice of a nation.

How else could this modern country, Germany, on the forefront of 1930s sophistication, culture, and technology turn so suddenly on their own countrymen to become a place of condoned ethnic targeting, and ultimately, extermination? What became of the society once made up of world-renowned physicians, scholars, musicians, and lawyers? What of the younger generation that had just begun swing dancing in the local ballrooms? Did they not see thousands of their Jewish neighbors packed into cattle cars everyday, never to return? How could this nation, a bastion of intellectual modernity, allow its reason to suddenly go awry, replaced by a movement to rid itself of the Jews? To understand the fever that raised this mass of hatred and complacency in German society, one must reconsider the common structures of that society as potential facilitators of the events that followed. In the *Fundamentals of Information Studies,* Lester and Koehler, Jr. (2003) wrote that:

> In a political sphere, information is used to influence behavior of citizens...to shape public opinion on national issues, and to inform and support public policy decisions. In this arena both the provision of information and the withholding of information are used as elements of control. p. 6

---

[41] Louis L. Snyder. Encyclopedia of the Third Reich. (New York, NY: Paragon House, 1989) 429-430.

In many ways, these same fundamentals speak to the elements of political propaganda that were perfected by the Nazis. In order to disseminate a lasting message of white supremacy, savvy propagandists try to utilize all elements of media that can be accessed by the intended audience. Anything short of this would leave room for opposition, logic, doubt, and dismissal. Hitler understood this well when he formed the Ministry for Public Enlightenment and Propaganda. This central division of the Nazi party was headed by Joseph Goebbels, Hitler's second in command. Under his direction, the Ministry became the essential tool of Nazi fanaticism as it systematically used media-based propaganda in horrific, yet groundbreaking ways.

The Propaganda Ministry was divided into seven departments intended to oversee every sphere of German culture; "Literature, news media, radio, theatre, music, visual arts, cinema."[42] In this way, the Nazis were able to completely restructure the nation's media into an authoritarian system. According to the United States Holocaust Memorial Museum, Hitler also understood the mobilizing power of household media devices, rather than just relying on traditional political billboards, rallies and speeches. As such, the radio became the primary means for uniting Germany under one Nazi banner:

> The Nazis were aware that the radio was the most efficient propaganda vehicle. Thus, inexpensive radio sets ("people's receivers")...were sold or distributed without cost. Between 1933 and 1941, the proportion of German families owning a radio rose from 25 percent to 65 percent.[43]

Once the Nazis had gained firm control of media structure in Germany, centralizing it into one arm of government, they needed to harness the social dependency on that structure via a message design that would shape the public opinion. The dis-

---

[42] John Dornberg. Munich 1923: The Story of Hitler's First Grab for Power. (New York, NY: Harper & Row, Publishers, 1982) 49-55.
[43] United States Holocaust Memorial Museum. "Der Sturmer." USHMM Propaganda Collection: Gift of the Museum fur Deutsche Geschichte, Berlin.

pensing of public radios certainly aided this cause, but 'device dependency' alone would not be enough to sow the seeds of an all out anti-Semitic movement across the country. For this, the propaganda itself had to be refined. The message had to be personalized to play on the fears of the people, rather than addressing politics alone. As such, the final stage of Hitler's takeover of public opinion occurred at the interpersonal level of mass communication through the social response to the propaganda messages. Noelle-Neumann's (1991) *Spiral of Silence* theory explains how this happens at the psychological stage of public opinion making.[44]

The essential basis behind Spiral of Silence posits that individuals tend to align their opinions with the general consensus of society out of fear of isolation and ostracism from the majority. When this phenomenon occurs, it is believed that "individuals will express opinions and behave in ways that they know are wrong in order to avoid social censure and criticism and to remain part of the crowd."[45] Rabkin (2000) concluded that Spiral of Silence phenomenon is only a "characteristic of controlled societies (like Communist or Nazi dictatorships) rather than of modern democracies."[46] He further noted that Noelle-Neumann began her own academic career as an assistant to later Nazi propagandist Joseph Goebbels, and she therefore saw the Spiral of Silence phenomenon unfold subjectively before her own eyes.

From a scholarly standpoint, these points suggest that the Spiral of Silence is based only on observations made of the most extreme totalitarian societies like Nazi Germany. However, while such criticisms might derail some of the theory's wider assertions,

---

[44] Elisabeth Noelle-Neumann. "Spiral of Silence Theory." In Katherine Miller's 2005 Communication Theories: Perspectives, Processes, and Contexts. (New York, NY: McGraw-Hill Companies, Inc., 1991).

[45] Katherine Miller. Communication Theories: Perspectives, Processes, and Contexts. (New York, NY: McGraw-Hill Companies, Inc., 2005) 277.

[46] Jeremy Rabkin. "Philosophizing Public Opinion." Public Interest, 14, (2000), 120-125.

Noelle-Neumann's work applies accurately to research on modern day hate speech in cyberspace which uses very similar techniques to build upon public fears of the "outsiders" in society. And this is precisely where the informational component of propaganda comes into play. The notion of being on the right side of an issue is essential to stoking fears of ostracism within a society, or a community, or simply a conversation for that matter. Typically, people want to be part of the informed group of society, and in the majority. Had the Nazis framed their initial message as openly bigoted in nature, or given the impression that they were in fact promoting genocide, their nationalist movement would have been exposed as tyrannical extremism, which of course it was. Instead, however, Nazi propagandists, like many of today's hate websites, strategically chose to speak in the languages of science, history, politics, economics, and nationalism. Within all these various intellectual themes, the Nazi's underlying message remained consistent. There was the right side of a national issue, based in facts and logic, and then there was the wrong side, based in Jewish lies and conspiracies, as identified by the Ministry's propaganda machine. The constant repetition of this message played a major role in conforming German society into quiet compliance.

Herf (2006) cites several of the methods by which the Ministry of Public Enlightenment and Propaganda was able to craft such an intellectually-based case for socially accepted anti-Semitism. They included inundating press offices with *Word of Day* directives (talking points about the Jews) to fill the pages of daily newspapers, crafting "pseudopsychology" to bolster scientific claims about the mental inferiority of Jews, blacks, gypsies, homosexuals, and other undesirables, and doctoring together "official statistics" of the Third Reich to paint a picture of a "supposed Jewish domination of German professional life" (p. 36). All of these falsities were carefully supported by seemingly legitimate sources ranging from newly appointed university professors to emerging anti-Semitic think tanks and countless intellectual journals suddenly dedicated to addressing the single academic conundrum, *Die Judenfrage* (The Jewish Question). And while the new scholars of Nazism were imposing the 'Jewish Question' upon all of German society, the Ministry of Public Enlightenment and Propaganda was simultaneously working around the clock to supply them with the answers.

For everyday German citizens, most of the titles upon their local newsstands appeared as they were before the media takeover, some had disappeared, but now the headlines had subtly changed – and so had their message. Within every news story about the Jews of Germany or greater Europe, a strong binary discourse was present. The theme of 'us versus them' was blatantly interlaced into the subtext of national news items, suggesting to all non-Jewish readers that they had to be on either one side of this equation or the other. And who was going to argue with the new science of race, or the rediscovered history of Aryan greatness, or the facts that proved the existence of a Jewish conspiracy, or the mob that reinforced it all?

White Nationalists and the Bright Future for Propaganda

For those who went on to study the effects of propaganda, both scholars and racists alike, much was learned from the tactics of the Ministry of Public Enlightenment and Propaganda. American research centers like the Institute for Propaganda Analysis were able to identify seven powerful techniques of mass persuasion. Of these seven, three practices – the *testimonial*, *transfer*, and *card stacking* techniques – reflected the false-informational role of propaganda that would become refined and mastered by new white supremacists in the coming years. The testimonial method would "rely upon the opinions of respected people to shape an audience," while transfer technique "carries the authority, sanction and prestige of something respected and revered," and lastly, card stacking involved "the selection and use of facts or falsehoods, illustrations or distractions...in order to give the best or the worst possible case."[47]

---

[47] Alfred C. Lee and Elizabeth B. Lee. The Fine Art of Propaganda. (New York: Harcourt, Brace and Co., Inc., 1939).

Collectively, these techniques borrow the opinions, authority and prestige of respected citizens and institutions of society, and present select interpretations of their ideas in order to produce a false truth; in this case about race. In fact, these strategies have been employed now by white power ideologues in America for decades. Beginning with Willis Carto, one of the earliest white nationalists to emerge from the Civil Rights era, the gradual transformation of hate speech, from the burning cross to the published word, would continue all the way on to Donald Black and the birth of Stormfront.org.

Carto started his campaign in 1955 with a faux-political magazine called *Right: The Journal of Forward-Looking American Nationalism.*[48] According to Zeskind (2009), Willis Carto often wrote under the chosen pseudonym of E.L. Anderson, Ph.D., and contended that "Western Civilization had entered a period of decline as a result of a polluted gene pool" (p. 9). Specifically, Carto was referring to African Americans whom he feared "might ultimately kill the American (white) culture." In a sense, Carto created his own testimonial device in the *Right* by inventing the academic voice, E.L. Anderson, Ph.D., to shape the opinions of his readers. Later, Carto formed a small anti-minority special interest group called the Liberty Lobby that became loosely associated with the Republican Party. In this way, Carto also attempted to transfer the authority and prestige of an American political party to strengthen his own initiative. While Carto was only briefly successful in his mainstream political pursuits, he did build a legacy of devout white nationalists, like himself, and a publishing company called the Noontide Press which later became dedicated to producing Holocaust denial literature. His objective to fight American multiculturalism on intellectual grounds would ultimately be followed by others.

Like Carto, William Pierce made a major impact on the white nationalist scene through literature when he published *The*

---

[48] Leonard Zeskind. Blood and Politics: The History of the White Nationalist Movement from the Margins to the Mainstream. (New York: Farrar, Straus and Giroux, 2009).

Turner Diaries in 1978, a novel depicting a domestic race war on American soil. Unlike Carto, however, Pierce's intellectual background was not invented and he used his academic legitimacy to propel his standing among the neo-Nazi movement that was rebuilding in the U.S. and Europe in the 1970s. Pierce earned his Ph.D. in physics from the University of Colorado and later taught at Oregon State University until he became a senior research scientist for an aerospace firm.[49] However, the career that Pierce ultimately settled on was as head of the National Alliance, an international neo-Nazi organization. There, according to Swain and Nieli (2003), Pierce would invent new means for spreading his underlying view "that nonwhites and Jews constitute an alien racial presence in America" (p. 261).

Key to Pierce's method was his ability to craft racist literature like *The Turner Diaries,* or his later work, *Hunter,* "which depicts the assassination of interracial couples and Jews" (p. 260). Although these were only works of fiction, the message behind their content was clear: racial war. Through published literature, Pierce continued Carto's strategy of legitimizing their cause along an intellectual line. *The Turner Diaries,* in particular, had wild success among the "racist right in Europe" where it was translated into French and German, as well as in the United States, where it has achieved a "cult status" among supremacists and militia groups alike. The popular book opens with a band of white revolutionaries using a homemade fertilizer bomb to blow up a federal building. *The Turner Diaries* has been cited as the inspirational text of many racist and antigovernment radicals, including Timothy McVeigh.[50] In 1995, McVeigh blew up an actual federal building in Oklahoma City using a homemade fertilizer bomb, killing 168 people.

---

[49] Carol M. Swain and Russ Nieli. Contemporary Voices of White Nationalism in America. (Cambridge, UK: Cambridge University Press, 2003) 260-261

[50] "Timothy McVeigh: Convicted Oklahoma City Bomber." Retrieved on August 12, 2009, from http://archives.cnn.com/2001/US/03/29/profile.mcveigh/.

If anyone followed the lessons of Pierce's *Turner Diaries* and Carto's Liberty Lobby, it was David Duke. Duke, too, understood early on that published prowess and political standing were the keys to "transferring" legitimacy to the white nationalist movement in America. He sought to obtain both. The Anti-Defamation League (ADL) has called David Duke "perhaps America's most well-known racist and anti-Semite."[51] A published white supremacist, Duke began his career in hate much like his predecessors, circulating newsletters like *The Racialist* on college campuses. However, Duke would make a much larger impact on the white nationalist scene as the founder, and later Grand Wizard, of the Knights of the Ku Klux Klan (a faction of the KKK) where he published several works like *The Crusader*. More importantly, Duke was very instrumental in the white power movement's resurgence in the 1970s because, according to the ADL, he was "one of the first neo-Nazi and Klan leaders to stop the use of Nazi and Klan regalia and rituals, as well as other traditional displays of race hatred, and to cultivate media attention." Duke's goal was to present himself as a "respectable racist," and the white nationalist movement to which he belonged, as a legitimate cause.

So successful was Duke in juxtaposing the themes of white supremacy with political race issues, like affirmative action, that he gained a large mainstream following in his home state of Louisiana. In 1989, Duke's ambition to evolve white nationalism into a common cause of the people was realized when he was elected the Republican State Representative of Louisana. According to Swain and Nieli (2003), David Duke's victory stunned the Republican political establishment, "from President George Bush...on down" (p. 166). Nevertheless, Duke, the recognized racist and anti-Semite had earned himself and the white power movement a genuine seat at the table of American politics. Duke would later lose other political elections, including a bid for Republic Party presidential candidate in 1992, but he would never

---

[51] "David Duke." Retrieved on August 1, 2009, from http://www.adl.org/learn/ext_us/david_duke/default.asp.

forget his strategic origins. Today, Duke has returned to the "intellectual" route, publishing in several formats and speaking at numerous "academic" conferences around the world on issues of personal interest to him like Holocaust denial. However, with regard to the future of white nationalism, Duke's lasting legacy may not rest at his own podium, but rather at the computer-savvy hands of his longtime protégé, Don Black.

Don Black started his career as a white nationalist in Alabama following in the footsteps of William Pierce. According to Zeskind (2009), Black joined the Knights of the Ku Klux Klan in 1975 and under the new tutelage of David Duke (p. 94). He ascended rapidly in Klan stature to become a Grand Dragon (state leader), and later, replaced his mentor David Duke as the Grand Wizard of the KKK (national director). But it was not until Don Black went to prison that he would realize his true potential as a modern voice for hate. Swain and Nieli chronicle the event in 1981 when Black and other Klan members "were arrested in a bizarre plot to invade the tiny Caribbean nation of Dominica in support of anticommunist forces on the island" (p. 153). Black was sent to a Texas federal penitentiary where he "made good use of his time there – Black first learned how to program computers in federal prison." Upon his release, Black returned to David Duke's side and the movement to normalize the face of white nationalism, but he never stopped experimenting behind the home computer. Like other social movements in the 1990s, Don Black recognized that the future of his own cause was somehow linked to this new computer technology. In 1995, Black launched the first white nationalist website from his Florida home called Stormfront.org. In his own words, he recalls:

> It was with the exponential growth of the Internet, which began, I think, in 94' or '95, that we first had the opportunity to reach potentially millions of people with our point of view. These are people who, for the most part, have never attended one of our meetings or have never subscribed to any of our publications. We were for the first time able to reach a broad audience. p. 155

And with that broad audience, Stormfront and the Internet wave carried the white power movement onto a new plain of public access. It was not long before underground books like the *Protocols of the Elders of Zion* and *The Turner Diaries* began to resurface on the web, while other white power publishers gained an immediate foothold by building their own websites and links to existing domains like Stormfront. In this way, the road to legitimizing hate had come full circle. What began with an ultimately exposed system of racist propaganda reinvented itself along a 50-year pathway through college campuses and publishing houses, faux-news journals and political lobbies, to political party status and elected legitimacy.

We should, at this moment in history, pause to pose a question about the transformational process of propaganda. Was the success of racial propagandists over this time period credited to gradual changes in technology, or was information itself the transformational hero of hate speech pioneers? One could argue that the explosion of media technologies in the latter half of the 20th century paved wider roads for fringe-based extremists to merge through new audio, video, and later digital access points. Others might conclude that the nature of information itself had changed and that its new meaning encompassed a greater diversity in sources, less exclusive, more inclusive over time. In fact, in the end, information and media technology scholars would argue that it was both. Lester and Koehler, Jr. (2003) write:

> The Internet, and more particularly the World Wide Web, have added a dimension of community to communications. Information technologies, where we are talking about oral communication and memory, the book, or the Internet redefine and sometimes replace the context in which the information they carry is interpreted. p. 149

The new contexts of information technology allowed, over time, the white power movement to redefine and replace itself with a new identity of sorts; one that shared not only the same spaces of the media (i.e., books and websites) as legitimate information sources, but also similar themes (i.e., politics and social issues). But, like the *Protocols of the Elders of Zion,* there is only one problem with the new legitimatized identity of white nationalism. It is only an illusion – an alias. In some ways, that makes little difference to white power organizations which can benefit from the evolving informational spaces either way.

James von Brunn, for instance, used the illusion of white power legitimacy to make a living under the employment of a Holocaust revisionist (denial) book publishing company. Later, he used the Internet to publish his own propagandist book, *Kill the Best Gentiles!,* a legacy he left behind before committing his deadly action at the Holocaust museum. Incidentally, the publishing house that employed von Brunn for years was Willis Carto's Noontide Press. This, of course, is no coincidence. It only demonstrates that simply obtaining standing in the information community does not sanctify the material of hate or its inscribers, although the David Dukes of the world are currently betting on the fact that it will.

In the next section, this research will show exactly how cyberspace, as an informational center, has delivered to the white power movement a new dimension for transforming the medium of racial propaganda. In the mid-1990s, such research on hate speech in cyberspace would have been both premature and highly inconclusive. Even though websites like Stormfront.org were quickly followed by others, the World Wide Web had not yet taken its full shape and little could be inferred, let alone understood, about where the new media would take the white power movement. However, in many ways we are beginning to see how the chips have fallen. As such, it is appropriate at this point to take a step forward toward understanding how today the white power movement has adapted itself into cyberspace. We begin by positing a new paradigm for explaining what the Internet has done for information and what that, in turn, has done for hate speech.

A New Theory of Information Laundering

In their research on "White Supremacists, Oppositional Culture and the World Wide Web,"[52] Adams and Roscigno speculated that the "growth of hate-oriented websites likely stems from a variety of conditions" (p. 763). Chief among them they cite the Internet as being a "relatively cheap and efficient tool for disseminating organizational information/propaganda to a mass audience," as well as providing a "free space" with limited media and political constraint." They also noted how "these sites assign specific meanings to current and past events, providing ideological reinterpretations of contemporary issues." Adams and Roscigno's 2005 study helped researchers to recognize three tangible elements by which hate groups have effectively used the Internet thus far to broaden their own agendas in "identity building, grievance framing and efficacy."

This research now aims to expand upon theirs and other existing theories of propaganda by offering the possibility of another factor that has helped to solidify a permanent place for fringe elements in cyberspace. That is the legitimizing factor of an interconnected information superhighway of web directories, research engines, news outlets, and social networks that collectively funnel into and out of today's hate websites. For information-seekers, the result of this funneling process is a wider array of perspectives, and thus, a broader understanding of any given topic. However, for propaganda-providers like the white power movement, the same process inadvertently lends the credibility and reputation of authentic websites to those illegitimate few to which they are nonetheless connected. Such is the case with many of today's leading search engines like Google, that unwittingly filter directly into hate websites, or public networks like YouTube which host their venomous content everyday. This theoretical process we call *information laundering* is unique to the

---

[52] Josh Adams and Vincent J. Roscigno. "White Supremacists, Oppositional Culture and the World Wide Web." Social Forces, 84:2, (2005) 759-777.

elements of cyberspace which provides the ideal media environment through which false information and counterfeit movements can be washed clean by a system of advantageous associations.

However, before we break this theory down by its various
processes and specific examples, it is important to examine two
theoretical building blocks of information laundering. These
concepts have helped to explain how propaganda and false information are sometimes overlooked, and even authenticated, by
the most educated of minds and reputable gatekeepers. The
theories of *white propaganda* (Jowett and O'Donnell, 1999)[53] and
academic/technical ethos (Borrowman, 1999)[54] follow a long line of
scholarly pursuits in the field of propaganda, some of which we
have already discussed. But these two contributions, in particular, lend a current perspective to the modified nature of propaganda in the information age.

Jowett and O'Donnell define propaganda as a highly functional communicative device that is "associated with control and
is regarded as a deliberate attempt to alter or maintain a balance
of power that is advantageous to the propagandist" (p. 15). In
terms of an analytical spectrum upon which to classify hate
speech in cyberspace, Jowett and O'Donnell's "Model of Propaganda" demonstrates the separation of information and persuasion according to purpose. This model illustrates a split in the
communication process between these two forces whereby
propaganda exists somewhere in between and often by design,
thus going unnoticed by the receiver. Jowett and O'Donnell call
this method *white propaganda* under the three distinctions white,
gray, and black (from selective facts to outright fabrications). Our
research is concerned with the nature of white propaganda, specifically, which deliberately blurs the line of persuasion and information. The result of this clever distortion is a produced mes-

---

[53] Garth S. Jowett and Victoria O'Donnell. Propaganda and Persuasion. (Thousand Oaks, California: SAGE Publications, 1999).
[54] Shane Borrowman. "Critical Surfing: Holocaust Deniability and
Credibility on the Web." College Teaching, 47:2, (1999) 44-54.

sage that appears "reasonably close to the truth... [and is] presented in a manner that attempts to convince the audience that the sender is a 'good guy' with the best ideas and political ideology" (p. 16).

While gray propaganda delves deeper into more dishonest practices like false advertising, "spin" and statistics-tampering, black propaganda is the most recognized form demonstrated in amplified public deceits like those of the Nazi era. However, in today's media-savvy society, white propaganda might be the most destructive of the three because of its effective ability to penetrate mainstream issues. As noted, the white power movement has moved *away* from recognizable hate symbols and *toward* engaging more day-to-day news items like domestic politics and public affairs. On the surface, these areas provide extremists with fodder for their ongoing narratives of generalized distrust, anger, and fear of nonwhite Americans. On the Internet, these themes have been carefully sewn into white power website forums which are intended to read just like daily news feeds or online editorials.

When considered as units unto themselves, many of these news articles do bear elements of accurate information. However, when the same reader steps back for a moment to observe all the articles, editorials, and forums of a given hate website, it becomes clear that these individual units are really part of a bigger mechanism that continually feeds one race-based news story after another. In this context, these contents have been carefully selected, highlighted, and in some cases, stripped down by the inscriber to convey only a distinct racist point of view. Later, we will see how white power websites use a common methodology of white propaganda to penetrate their racist perspectives into the mainstream funnel of interconnected blogs, web encyclopedias, online bookstores, online news, search engines....and so on.

Like white propaganda, Borrowman's concept of an *academic* and *techno-ethos* also examines the manipulation of information through the media, but more specifically it considers the creditability-building qualities of this process in cyberspace. In his study on the educational pitfalls in cyberspace, Borrowman considers the example of students who use the Internet to research the Holocaust. He observes how through an open network, students could be led directly to Holocaust denial websites which are structured to appear as reputable research centers with professional titles, university affiliations, links to published literature, and academic-sounding mission statements. He explains:

> When academic ethos is at work, a reader is convinced that the writer is a rational, reasonable, intelligent individual who is engaging in an honest dialogue...readers are led to believe that a writer is being ethical and fair in the construction of his or her argument. For Holocaust deniers the construction of such an ethos is enormously important. (p.7)

Beyond the contextual methods for constructing the appearance of "an expert in a given field," Borrowman also asserts that a new *techno-ethos* has also evolved in cyberspace. He contends, "techno-ethos is the credibility or authority that is constructed online in the programming proficiency demonstrated in a flashy Web site." Today, this can be achieved with relative ease through either technical know-how or simply hiring a qualified website designer. The fruits of this labor can be extremely effective with the net generation whose critical thinking skills Borrowman fears have been partially replaced by what he calls "critical surfing." In other words, young researchers have become accustomed to giving credence to websites simply based on their professional designs, visual appeal, sophisticated options in media convergence, and the volume of its visitors.

With so many young adults assigning these features the mark of credible information, it should come as little surprise that so many white power groups are lining up to acquire the best website designers that money can buy. If we pause to recall a time not so long ago when trusted information was equated more so with tattered books on library bookshelves and scholarly journals, then it should seem strange that a new media could alter that valued system so abruptly. But as Borrrowman and others have observed, it has. However, the concepts of *academic* and *techno-ethos* only describe the *quality* of today's online research bases. These qualities, along with white propaganda, are critical elements to the theory of information laundering, but only to the extent that hate groups have learned to employ them inside of their own websites. The other half of that formula exists well beyond the homepage in the *pathway* that led to these illegitimate spaces. This all important external factor called "the information superhighway" was not created by the white power movement, but nevertheless it has become their most crucial accomplice.

In cyberspace, the pathways to false knowledge and propaganda are the same as those that lead to legitimate and credible resources. It is as if beneficiaries like the white power movement have slid into a new Dewey Decimal System and contaminated it, but few have noticed their presence there. Today, racist websites have become conveniently integrated and interconnected into the central pillars of information-providing. This research divides these pillars into four major categories: search engines (discovery), research and news (information), blogs and politics (opinion), and social networks (expression).

Search Engines

Like most processes in cyberspace, a system of information laundering begins at the primary entrance point for most online research and day-to-day inquiries, the *search engine*. As the Internet has been gradually refined over the last ten years, so, too, have many of today's search engines. Today, the leaders of the field consistently include Google, Yahoo, Bing, Ask, and AOL, which are easily ranked among the most visited website domains in cyberspace.

A typical search engine designates the more relevant websites upfront in their directory pages usually based upon the "popularity" and "freshness" of these sites.[55] The more popular the space, the more likely it has appeal, and therefore, an assumed relevance to a large group of users. At the same time, certain web-

---

[55] Dirk Lewandowski. "Search engine user behavior: How can users be guided to quality content?" Information Services & Use, 28, (2008) 261-268.

sites might contain the most recent and, again, relevant input, regardless of their prominence. Such sites are considered "fresh" and can quickly be allocated to a higher ranking in the results pages. Other factors that determine search engine relevancy include a website's location with regard to the user's server, the breadth of the query itself (the scope of information sought), existing business agreements between search engine and website, most notably Google and Wikipedia, and other emerging factors. Once again, this same process has also worked to the benefit of websites that are less-than-reputable when it comes to the information they provide, but are nonetheless either popular among a large group of users or current in terms of the kinds of content they offer relating to a given topic, or, they might simply be close in namesake to the search terms entered by the user.

The web information company, Alexa.com, which tracks the "traffic metrics" of activity in cyberspace, also details the "clickstream" for every given website noting the immediate pathway that led a user into that particular site.[56] While the leading hate sites examined in this study are frequently funneled into via other racist websites, Alexa has cited consistently their number one preceding page was Google, followed closely by Yahoo.

Research and News

The *research and news* pathway often represents the second stop for information-seekers in cyberspace. Depending upon the nature of the investigation, and of course, the investigator, a news and research conduit like CNN.com can create an important buffer between an informative source and the hate website it references. On the other hand, some research and news content can be as random as search engine results. Public encyclopedias like Wikipedia are a prime example of this potential because their content can be inscribed or altered by just about anyone

---

[56] Alexa Web Information. Retrieved on August 20, 2009, from http://alexa.com/.

and, further, they provide direct links to the topics they reference, including white power websites.

While websites like Wikipedia and CNN might differ in the
level of their accuracy in information (the former is a public-
driven website while the latter is professionally-inscribed), we
must remember that online users may or may not make this distinction for themselves. The underlying parallel between these
two sites is that they provide information which is *assumed* accurate and useful by the net generation in particular. Another example of such a site that offers 'legitimacy by association' is
Amazon.com. For many Internet users, like college students,
Amazon is their premiere source for books. But as a trusted provider of informative resources, Amazon's variety of literature also
includes titles ranging from *The Protocols* to *The Turner Diaries*. Of
course, these can be relevant documents for anyone pursuing this
kind of research. However, the danger of discovery in Amazon is
that younger shoppers can arrive at these works of literature in
quest of other legitimate resources that may bear related search
terms but non-related topics. The Southern Poverty Law Center
noted Amazon users that "punch 'Klan' into the book search
engine...pull up to a staggering 22,767 results" relating to the
Ku Klux Klan.[57]

These kinds of academic inquiries negotiate an on-going
struggle between the legitimate providers of information and the
hate-filled agencies that infiltrate their venues of research, literature, and occasionally, even the mainstream news. Such was the
case with Fox News that, twice in 2008, booked racist guests on
programs where they were then identified as an "Internet journalist" and "free speech activist."[58] The "Internet journalist,"
Andy Martin, had appeared on "Hannity's America" to talk
about then-Senator Obama's conspiratorial association with

---

[57] Mark Potok. "Books on the Right." Retrieved on August 20, 2009,
from http://www.splcenter.org/intel/intelreport/article.jsp?aid=904
(2008)
[58] "Extremism in the Media." Retrieved on August 20, 2009, from
http://www.splcenter.org/intel/intelreport/article.jsp?aid=1007

convicted terrorist William Ayers, but had also been known in
litigious circles as an outspoken racist. The ADL had followed
Martin's history of "filing literally hundreds of lawsuits" marked
in phrases like "crooked, slimy Jew" and sentiments like "I am
able to understand how the Holocaust took place, and with every
passing day feel less and less sorry that it did." Fox News would
later apologize for accidentally legitimizing their anti-Semitic
guests. However, for the white power movement, these incidences, along with references on Wikipedia and rising book sales
on Amazon, signify successful penetrations onto the mainstream
information stage.

Blogs and Politics

From news and research, we move to the next level of infor-
mation-gathering on the World Wide Web. The *blogs and politics*
category represents the much broader sphere of less constrained
civic journalism on the Internet. Certainly less professional than
news and research in terms of its gatekeepers, the blogosphere as
it has come to be known is far more concerned with the opinions
of everyday people than with the facts and drawn conclusions of
experts and reporters.

By far, the grayest area of information in cyberspace, the
blogosphere is a venue for citizens to share their perspectives and
feelings about political and social issues, and from which other
users can examine those perspectives to form their own opinions.
Like public encyclopedias, blogs and political pages are easily
arrived at through the initial search engine inquiry. However, in
terms of trusted information, a greater degree of separation exists
between the filters of news and research and the vast medley of
the online editorials and public debate pages that collectively
constitute this entity called the blogosphere.

For the white power movement, this gray area poses even
greater opportunities to breach the intellectual pursuits of those
same everyday people. The journey into the fringe element of
cyberspace often runs through these corridors of public debate
that speak to issues of legitimate political and social concern, but

can be exploited by hate groups all the same who need not identify their affiliations with white power extremes. Within true examples of the blogosphere, all opinion pages are open forums unto which other readers may respond with their own comments, and provide links to further online readings.

Some white power blogs feed off other arenas of political debate, such as those found on rightwing or leftwing websites dedicated to one particular issue. For instance, the Israeli-Palestinian conflict has given birth to literally thousands of political blogs all over the world. However, select elements of the white power movement have zeroed in on this debate in order to capitalize on its politics, and inject their own sentiments of religious intolerances against Jews, Muslims, or both, depending on their platform. Other white supremacist inscribers use blogs the same way they do online bookstores – to open doorways to the direct sources of intolerance via links or outright promotions of hate group websites and organizations.

Social Networks

Finally, the growing universe of *social networks* in cyberspace has begun to provide the white power movement with an informational segue into the mainstream youth culture. More than just a friend-building network, social sites have recently become their own peripheral venues for the blossoming of political and cultural expression. Like all other opportunities, the white power movement has quickly honed in on this new prospect. Earlier examples of this phenomenon include the growing Facebook community of Holocaust deniers that provide links and literature on the "Jewish lie" of the Nazi's genocide, as well as emerging "White pride" groups that use social networks in attempts to educate fellow members on the threats of nonwhite America. Yet, in addition to building the latest cyber pathway into racist subculture, mainstream social networks have inadvertently supplied the white power movement with something far more valuable than just another platform from which to convey messages of hate or links to their source. They deliver the net generation.

There is no more concentrated category of the Internet than social networking websites to attract the prime audience whom the white power movement is so desperately striving to recruit. The college crowd that fills the pages of sites like Facebook and MySpace are no doubt the target recipients of those same white power groups that are well-aware of their "favorite places" in cyberspace. This particular crowd, culture, and social network will be the prime subject of the next chapter. Along with content-sharing websites like Napster and YouTube, which have also unintentionally opened up their gateways to racist materials, social networks have given the white power movement a direct feed into the minds and interests of the net generation.

For our purposes here, the social networks represent the last piece of the white supremacist's puzzle needed to achieve their own fluid network for sustaining a permanent place in cyberspace. The result of funneling through these four pillars of discovery, information, opinion, and expression can be seen in the recent mainstream surfacing of racist sentiments and the concurrent rise in the number of hate websites on the Internet. Through this opportune system of associations – some cleverly acquired, and others by sheer happenstance – the white power movement is able to digitally launder hateful rhetoric through the Internet channels in order to produce a loose form of accepted public knowledge.

Figure 2.1 *Model of Information Laundering in Cyberspace*

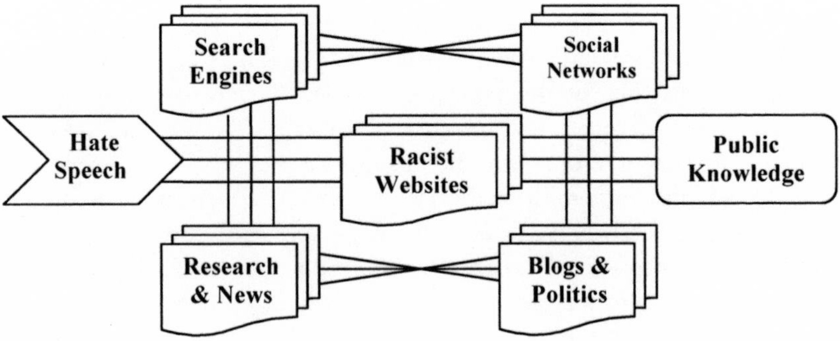

Today, this process is playing out in cyberspace everyday without public awareness or media investigation about where certain mainstream racist sentiments originated. For instance, accusations about a president's religion or claims about his nationality do not emerge from true academic, political, or public debates. Rather, they begin on the fringes, in white power websites, and only through the Internet where they have found a successful pathway to work racist themes into mainstream issues. This research, and in particular, the later content analysis, aims to intercept and locate these messages of hate at their root. The white power websites, being one strand of racial propaganda, contained several recurring sentiments, or frames, of extremism. Some of these frames have been already absorbed by mainstream view-dispensers like media analysts and political pundits, while others have yet to surface.

However, before this research extends deeper into that later analysis of racial hate at the source, let us briefly consider this experiment in the pathway that we call information laundering. As a preliminary test, this research entered four keywords into four leading search engines. The search terms Holocaust, Islam, White people, and Black people were typed into the Google, Yahoo, Bing, and Ask.com search engines, and only the first three pages of results were reviewed. From this basic observational approach, all four search engines yielded at least two results that were sponsored by white supremacist websites or racist inscribers.

On their first page of its results, Google listed a link to a webpage about "black people," which immediately led to another page containing ugly racial slurs and hateful jokes.[59] On their second page of results for "white people," the search engine giant had a direct listing for a National Socialist website that con-

---

[59] Google search: "Black People." Retrieved on August 20, 2009, from http://www.google.com/search?sourceid=navclient&ie=UTF-8&rlz=1T4RNWI_enUS280US280&q=black+people

tained inner-links to Holocaust revisionist (denial) information.[60] Both Bing and Yahoo offered listings on their pages for anti-Islamic websites[61],[62] which denigrated both the religion and the Muslim people, while Ask.com presented the "Holocaust Hoax" website within its set of otherwise legitimate results.[63] Other search results included direct links to the White Revolution homepage, a separatist organization, and several "black joke" websites. It is important to note that within many of these initial hits one finds links to other white power websites even more virulent than the first, thereby threading together in just one or two moves the fringe elements of cyberspace to a mainstream search engine.

Conclusion

There are no perfect formulas for explaining the lasting power of racist propaganda in society. The theory of information laundering only attempts to explain *this* generation's version of that toxic phenomenon, but as we have seen, expressions of organized bigotry adapt with the times. From *The Protocols* forgery, contrived in Russia but circulated throughout the world, to the *Turner Diaries*, inscribed in Virginia but later carried out in Oklahoma City, the effects of information-driven hate speech can be contagious and permanent. As students of media and information, we can try to comprehend patterns of propaganda that have

---

[60] Google search: "White People." Retrieved on August 20, 2009, from http://www.google.com/search?hl=en&source=hp&q=black+people&aq=f&oq=&aqi=g-z1g9

[61] Bing search: "Islamic." Retrieved on August 20, 2009, from http://www.bing.com/search?q=Islam&first=21&FORM=PERE1

[62] Yahoo search: "Islamic." Retrieved on August 20, 2009, from http://search.yahoo.com/search?p=Islam&ei=UTF-8&fr=yfp-t-150&pstart=1&b=21

[63] Ask search: "Holocaust." Retrieved on August 20, 2009, from http://www.ask.com/web?q=Holocaust&qsrc=0&frstpgo=0&o=0&l=dir&qid=97C2C68CC46ADFACE2E38AC40D32A2CA&page=3&jss=1

endured over time the same way that military historians collect reoccurring clues about warring civilizations. In this light, we can begin to see how, since the advent of mass communication, racist opportunists have managed to manipulate the structures of information dependency in society, to their own ends. The two variables of this equation – media systems and the next generation – are always changing. But if yesterday has taught us anything, it is that hate groups have an eerie ability to keep up with both.

3. Recruiting the Ne(x)t Generation

The net generation was born into the age of cyberspace. Today they use the Internet for everything from communicating with friends to finding romance, watching movies to posting their own, shopping for cars to downloading books and music, and from time to time, they also check in with the family. For almost every application of external society, the net generation has been brought up with the convenient 'e-version' of that same function. In his 2004 study of "Net-geners between the ages of 16 and 24," Leung found that 38% of those surveyed could be classified as "Internet addicts," according to Young's (1996) definition,[64] because they were spending 38 hours a week or more on the web and *outside* of time spent on work, school, family and friends.[65] That means that for many young adults, nearly one-fourth of their day is being spent in some realm of cyberspace, from online gaming to chat rooms and everything in between. In that sense, it is almost impossible to deny that the Internet will have a monumental impact on this next generation's collective development and world view.

A typical day in the life of an 18-year-old college student might resemble any number of online routines and rituals depending upon their interests. That young adult might begin his day by checking through various emails before he heads to class. If there is time, he reads a few headlines from his daily news website of choice, or reviews messages on a social network of which he is a member. Later, he views a "must-see" video he heard about on YouTube, where he is already one of 800,000 people to see the posting. Then he consults Wikipedia to double-check an answer he gave on a test. By noon, he reads over the

---

[64] Kimberly S. Young. "Internet addiction: The emergence of a new clinical disorder." CyberPsychology & Behavior, 1, (1996) 237-244.
[65] Louis Leung. "Net-Generation Attributes and Seductive Properties of the Internet as Predictors of Online Activities and Internet Addiction." CyberPsychology & Behavior, 7:3, (2004) 333-348.

news site once again, but this time the headline has changed (and
so, too, has the concept of 'headline news'). Later, he uses a library database to pull up a few articles. For his assignment, he
decides to consult Wikipedia once again, but this time the information he receives is inaccurate, unbeknownst to him. At the end
of the day, homework begins, but so, too, does the barrage of
instant messages, music downloads, online gaming, and one final
visit to his email before heading to bed around 2am.

Of course this is just a dramatization, but one that is not so
far from reality. And while this routine may seem alarming, we
will soon discover that today's net generation is far from out-of-
touch with the world. In fact, they are keyed into it as early as
age six in ways that previous generations were not, and by many
accounts, are even more globally-oriented than their predecessors. What *is* alarming about their online routine is how overwhelming it has become relative to their everyday lives, and
therefore, not balanced by necessary real life experience – the
kind that can later help form judgments about certain online
contents and decisions. However, in addition to problems of
overuse, the online routine of the net generation is also overrun
with mass commercialism as well as other more sinister exploiting elements that have mastered the art of replication.

The typical day in the life of a white power ideologue in cyberspace begins and ends much the same as that of the 18-year-
old college student, and there is no doubt, this is by design. A
young adult who has been drawn to the racist fringes of cyberspace, either by choice or by accident, might spend his morning
surfing the pages of the New Saxon – a social networking site
"for whites by whites" by its own account.[66] From there, he
moves on to the latest news updates from the Vanguard News
Network or VNN (motto: No Jews. Just Right).[67] Later, the white
power pupil might link into the Podblanc video-sharing website.

---

[66] New Saxon. "An online community for whites by whites." Retrieved
June 20, 2009, from http://newsaxon.org/
[67] Vanguard News Network. Retrieved June, 2009, from
http://www.vanguardnewsnetwork.com/

There, he views amateur anti-Semitic videos or even real life racial batteries uploaded from all over the world. For his daily inquiries, Metapedia.com offers encyclopedic input on all matters
of society, especially race. Finally, for leisure, the young racist
can shop for apparel at aryanwear.com, download music at Final
Stand Records, or play the online game "Border Patrol" where,
through the scope of a rifle, the intent is to shoot and kill Mexican women and children. And yes, there are even white singles
and dating forums which are frequented daily on Stormfront.org.

However, for all of its apparent blatancy and obvious exposure in this comparative context, the white power movement's
virtual image has begun to look, sound, and even to some degree,
read like many of today's popular youth culture websites. The
result of this virtual cloning process is evident in the new exterior
persona of the white power movement. What once was perceived
as transparent racism in the form of bonfire rallies and book-
burning parades has been carefully modified and adapted to mirror the popular trends and appearances of today's youth culture
in cyberspace. The result are hate websites like Stormfront that
appear to look more like Craigslist.

Figure 3.1 From *Stormfront.org*[68]

Welcome to the Stormfront.

If this is your first visit, be sure to check out the FAQ. You must register before you can post to any forum except those designated as open to guests. To start viewing messages, select the forum that you want to visit from the selection below

- Homemaking
  (20 Viewing) Domestic: gardening, cooking, child rearing, etc.
  Sub-Forums: Trades and Skills, Homesteading and Hobby Farming

- Education and Homeschooling
  (9 Viewing) Preparing ourselves and our children.

- Music and Entertainment
  (78 Viewing) Popular culture: music, movies, television.
  Sub-Forums: Movie Reviews, Musicians

- Science, Technology and Race (14 Viewing)
  Genetics, eugenics, racial science and related subjects.

- For Stormfront Ladies Only
  (19 Viewing) Sugar and spice, and everything nice

- Classified Ads
  (12 Viewing)
  Buy, Sell, Trade or Give Away

- Youth (18 Viewing)
  White Nationalist issues among teens.

- Dating Advice (9 Viewing)

- Talk (17 Viewing) Meet other White Nationalists for romance or friendship.

In this chapter, we will begin to examine one of the over-arching observations of this research: How keenly hate groups have understood and adapted to the media culture of this generation – something which we now know they have been doing for decades.

Better Understanding the Net Generation

So how did white supremacists reproduce such an accurate version of modern online culture? To better understand what many racial propagandists have learned themselves we must take the same journey they have into the mind of the net generation. In fact, some of the questions we ask here echo those constantly pondered by white supremacists. Questions like, in which types

---

[68] Stormfront. Retrieved May 15, 2009, from
http://stormfront.org/forum/

of media do teenagers and college kids most indulge online? Which social networking sites attract most users? What political issues speak to the interests of today's young academic visitor? What matters to them most? And where do their biggest concerns lie today?

Of course, there is no mystery behind the answer to the underlying question of "why." That is, why is the white power movement so interested in these and other youth-related topics? The answer is recruitment. As Reno Wolf, founder of the National Association for the Advancement of White People (NAAWP), asserted, "We get a lot of members off the Internet...In fact, we figured out that in the last couple of months, about 12 percent of those who visit our website really follow through and join the organization."[69] Matt Hale of the Creativity Alliance proudly declared, "We particularly attract the youth. In fact, I could say that half of our members are younger than twenty-five years old – we are a very youth-based organization...We attract college students mainly through the Internet" (Swain & Nieli, 2003).

The recruiting successes of Reno Wolf, Matt Hale, and countless other white supremacist organizers can best be attributed to their keen understanding of this generation's culture, their needs and interests, frustrations and fears. For our part, we can attempt to understand the net-gener's traits by considering a few commonalities among young online-users, as drawn from recent studies. Much like a modern screenwriter, we must first build a thorough character sketch of today's net generation before we can accurately tell their story.

In *Growing up digital: the rise of the net generation,* Tapscott (1998) constructs a thorough bio of today's young adult that also offers insights into some of their online behavior.[70] He portrays the net

---

[69] Carol M. Swain and Russ Nieli. Contemporary Voices of White Nationalism in America. (Cambridge, UK: Cambridge University Press, 2003) 114-132.

[70] Don Tapscott. Growing up digital: the rise of the Net Generation, (New York: McGraw-Hill, 1998)

generation as globally-oriented having grown up with the World
Wide Web, and at the same time, highly "assertive" and "uninhibited" within its anonymous environment. Their generation
believes strongly in a right to information and being given access
to explore it at an early age. They are undoubtedly a technology-
savvy group, "innovative and investigative." But net-geners also
"want options ... Accustomed to years of TV channel surfing
and Internet surfing, they expect a world of limitless choices" (p.
335). Finally, Tapscott concludes that this new group of adolescents is more preoccupied with adulthood and maturity than
most of their predecessors. This should come as little surprise
when one considers that the net generation has been exposed to
mature ideas and images in cyberspace when prior generations
were being steadily educated and entertained by more structured
media programs in the vein of PBS's Sesame Street.

However, the net generation's exposures to the Internet and
its windows into adulthood have not necessarily produced a more
independent group of young adults. In fact, many conclude just
the opposite. McAllister (2009)[71] asserts that this generation
whom she calls the Millennials are much more "sheltered" than
they are self-governing. She reminds us:

> This is the "Baby on Board" Generation. From birth, this gen-
> eration has taken a place of priority in the world. Parental con-
> trol can be found in car monitoring devices to their own Face-
> book accounts as a means of tracking their child's online activ-
> ity. In addition, teachers of this generation have found that
> parents are quick to come to their child's defense, often being
> dubbed "helicopter parents."

---

[71] Andrea McAlister. "Teaching the Millennial Generation." American
Music Teacher, 58:7, (2009) 13-15.

McAllister and others (Tapscott[72], 2008; Banschick & Ban-schick[73], 2003) also observed that Millennials are heavily team-oriented, adept at multitasking, and driven toward achievements.

Many studies of the past decade have drawn a similar sketch of the net generation. Collectively, these young adults represent somewhat of a paradox in their development. In one sense, they are given the control and privilege of navigating through a mature (media) world at an earlier phase of life. On the other hand, this same group which has thoroughly previewed a world which they are yet to join has also been more protected than previous generations, and as a result, underexposed to experiences that teach self-reliance beyond the digital securities they know so well. Only time will tell whether or not this is a good or a bad thing, but some psychologists already believe that virtual safeguards such as online anonymity will no doubt affect this generation's long-term development in one fashion or another.

In "Social and Psychological Uses of the Internet," Magdoff and Rubin (2003) examine the notion of identity-building in cyberspace.[74] They suggest that, online, "You can be anyone...New possibilities in the ways in which people posit their identities are being created by constant advances in computer technology." A prime example of this technological phenomenon can be found in the gaming world where kids of all ages often take on exaggerated personas, called avatars, and interact in real-time role-playing games with other avatars. These online games are certainly more anonymous and secure in ways that the playground simply is not. However, Magdoff and Rubin also suggest

---

[72] Don Tapscott. Growing up digital: How the Net Generation is changing your world, (New York: McGraw-Hill, 2008).

[73] Mark R. Banschick and Josephia J. Banschick. Children in Cyberspace. In Leonard Shyles' (Ed.) Deciphering Cyberspace: Making the Most of Digital Communication Technology. (Thousand Oaks, CA: Sage Publications, 2003) 159-199.

[74] JoAnn Magdoff and Jeffrey B. Rubin. "Social and Psychological Uses of the Internet." In Leonard Shyles' (ed.) Deciphering Cyberspace: Making the Most of Digital Communication Technology. (Thousand Oaks, CA: Sage Publications, 2003) 201-216.

that there can be fallbacks to this kind of cyber-interaction, despite its seemingly social nature. "Seeking to escape isolation, adolescents use the Internet as a transitional space between being alone and being physically with others. It can be great, but it can also result in perpetuating one's difficulties in living rather than resolving them" (p. 210).

The counter argument, of course, is that these developmental online interactions are actually preparing the net generation for their future interfaces in the real world. In the mean time, they will comfortably develop inside of their egg-like online environments while gradually expanding their reach into the adult world one website at a time. That same analogy, however, implies another possibility. While social development in cyberspace may seem safe from the inside, we now know that the Internet is a penetrable shell easily cracked by outside elements. For this reason, we examine not only the young Internet user, but also the online world that their participation has largely helped to create.

Online Youth Culture

In chapter 1, we conceptualized the World Wide Web as an "anything goes" environment where the young Internet user defines much of the predominant landscape with his or her contributions of culture. In chapter 2, we examined the central pillars of information in cyberspace through which the net generation constantly discovers new content, becomes informed, and arrives at opinions, or offers their own forms of expression. These, we noted, are easily-penetrated mediums through which the white power movement attempts to filter their illegitimate content and funnel users towards their own websites.

As a preamble to the research sections which follow, this chapter identifies those constructs of popular online youth culture which, like any media trend, are ever-changing. But a snapshot of the virtual environment today can already reveal much about the illegitimate elements that work feverishly to reproduce it, or penetrate and exploit its more popular websites. After all, web pages like Twitter and YouTube are not merely channels of online entertainment, but also a direct window into the lives and minds of the net generation that populate them.

So what does the online youth culture look like? Here, we define the constructs of young cyberspace into identifiable sub-cultures, or genres. Much like the television or music industry has its own media varieties that speak to the interests of young adults, so, too, does the Internet. The most popular online genres among today's younger generation are social networks, gaming, video-sharing and music download sites. In recent years, the net generation has become much more culturally attuned to politics as well, although as a virtual construct of cyberspace, political youth organization websites are far less frequented than the pages of iTunes or MySpace.

For the virtual outsider who is not a member of a social net-work like Facebook, MySpace, LinkedIn, Tagged, or Twitter, these websites probably seem like the next extension of the tele-phone. Far from it, these online centers are fully functional communities where members interact both publicly and privately by sharing friends, music, culture, games, homework, advice, and virtual life experiences. The atmosphere of a social network is one where the full exposure of private lives, opinions, pictures, and other personal content is embraced as the norm. On Face-book, for instance, it is perfectly acceptable to befriend a 'friend of a friend' with whom you have had no prior exchanges, just a picture profile. On Twitter, one is encouraged to "follow" people and organizations to which they have no associations, but none-theless publish personal comments about on a regular basis. And on LinkedIn, the young professional crowd is constantly prompted to mix business with pleasure in this occupationally-based social network. From time to time, these various interfaces can become too public for the user's comfort.

The world of online gaming is a media marriage between the premiere game software providers and the World Wide Web that feeds access to literally millions of "gamers" everyday. From as early as age six to players in their late 20s, the net generation is widely represented in this vast segment of Internet culture. Today, system providers like X-Box, Playstation, Wii, and various PC gaming companies have tapped into the creative and interactive minds of the net generation. In online gaming, we see a fantasy world played out among interconnected players socializing amid extremes of adventure and violence. Games like Halo, Call of Duty, and World of Warcraft have seemingly replaced both the video games of old and the outdoor adventures of adolescence, because in their own way, these online games have simulated the best of both worlds. A high-stakes game of Halo, for instance, can bring together dozens of kids, teenagers, and college students into one "party" where their characters play with or against each other while they converse along through audio connections. Gamers may spend hours in play, or simply socializing with other players from all over the country – friends whom they will never actually meet, but nonetheless get to know so well.

Video-sharing and music download websites collectively share two fundamental elements of online net-generational culture: content and expression. The premiere video-sharing website, YouTube, is a great example of how a single-purpose website can gradually morph into a multidimensional community of content and expression that no one expected it to become. On its face, video-sharing websites are an online base for amateur movies to be posted and seen by other users. But like the social networks that grew from profiles and pictures into community organizing and information sharing functions, video sites have also become a multifaceted medium for expressions of comedy, politics, faith, art, community, etc. The goal of many users who post content on video-sharing websites is to create an amateur sensation that will spread across cyberspace like virtual wildfire. For many political organizations, YouTube itself has become a new vehicle for disseminating their message in a more creative fashion.

Like video-sharing, music download sites house not only songs, albums, and artists, but also represent the multitude of expressions of today's net generation. Since the Roaring 20s, modern music has always been at the forefront of youth culture and today it is no different. Websites like Rhapsody and I-Tunes offer the net generation varying means for downloading musical content at low cost, or even freely, but they also provide online space for less established musicians to make a name for themselves. In this way, a growing number of musical outlets in cyberspace, including YouTube which is used to post amateur music videos, have collectively begun to create a more public-fed form of creative expression. Whereas for decades, leading forms of popular music and motion picture entertainment were strictly limited to commercial content that was driven by executive gatekeepers, the Internet culture has drawn an entire generation away from those traditional venders and toward a public source of online media.

Whether it is a matter of cultural expression represented by or created within these content-based websites, the driving force behind the successes of YouTube and I-Tunes alike is the same factor that fuels the sensation of online gaming and social networks – interactivity. The desire to produce one's *own* music video, political commentary, comedy skit, dance number, digital album, game map, or friend network, speaks to an additional characteristic of this net generation. That is their insistence on being an active participant and creator of their culture's content and expression rather than just the recipients of its traditionally-mediated forms. In a word, it is all about identity.

From the adult-like interactions found in social networks to the fantasies and role-playing of online gaming, to the creative films, music, and even generational causes expressed through content-sharing websites, the underlying theme in all these utilizations of young cyberspace is identity. In fact, for decades studies and theories have sought to understand the relation between the identities of media receivers, such as the net generation, and the potential success of the content-provider in reaching them. We have already considered some of these studies with regard to the effectiveness of propaganda, but there are other broader theories of media-reception that speak directly to the issue of cultural connections for specific types of mediated messages.

Bandura's (1962) *Social Learning Theory* is one of the most essential foundations for examining the personal relationships that exist between mass messages and consumer reception.[75] This significant theory challenged the original "hypodermic needle effect" that asserted transmission of a media message into an audience's psyche was a direct path. Such was seemingly the case with Nazi propaganda in the 1930s and 1940s. However, Bandura did not believe that mass media worked in such a penetrable fashion. To measure the response of an audience, he insisted, one could not simply ignore the audience itself. From his theory, Bandura began to explore those factors that led to the rejection of a message as well as its reception, a process he called "social learning." Among the many factors he posited, *identification* addressed the possibility that an individual consumer "feels a strong psychological connection to a model" of the media based on their own views and life experiences. As Miller (2005) later explained, "If [that consumer] feels a sense of identification with a model, social learning is likely to occur."[76]

In some ways, social learning theory might seem somewhat obvious to today's consumers of mass media, especially the net generation who naturally assume they play an important role in their own response to the content they absorb. However, this idea was groundbreaking during a time when many believed that media influence and social learning processes worked as fluent mechanisms of cause and effect, like the strings of a puppeteer. This was also a profound statement to make with regard to the everyday citizens of 1930s Germany who claimed, post-war, to have been duped by the propagandist ideology of the Nazi party. For those easily influenced by the white power movement, the social cognitive theory suggests that they, in fact, play an active

---

[75] Albert Bandura. "Social learning through imitation." In M.R. Jones (Ed.), Nebraska symposium on motivation (Vol. 10). (Lincoln: University of Nebraska Press, 1962)

[76] Katherine Miller. Communication Theories: Perspectives, Processes, and Contexts. (New York, NY: McGraw-Hill Companies, Inc., 2005) 224.

role in their own seduction process by culturally identifying with the message of white supremacy.

Today, some of the same principles of identification apply to hateful messages in cyberspace, though the modern Internet-user is without question part of a more media-savvy generation and overall diverse culture. In other words, for a white nationalist website to effectively align their content with a particular segment of online youth culture, they must build that same "strong psychological connection" in the form of their message and presentation. Assuming that the white power movement has created a successful model community in cyberspace – fully functional, informative, engaging, and user-friendly – the process of now attracting the young white generation relies heavily upon their strategies of recruitment. Like propaganda, recruitment methods have also been reconsidered and modified in recent years to fit the new media of the net generation.

Theories of Recruitment

In their 2006 work on "Persuasion Techniques Used on White Supremacists Websites," Weatherby and Scroggins adopted what they refer to as "compliance techniques" to describe the methods for online recruitment in white power culture.[77] Specifically, they applied the social psychological theories known as Foot-in-the-door[78] and Low-ball technique[79] to their analysis of organized hate websites. With foot-in-the-door technique, Weatherby and Scroggins reapply the principle that "a

---

[77] Georgie A. Weatherby and Brian Scroggins. "A Content Analysis of Persuasion Techniques Used on White Supremacist Websites." Journal of Hate Studies, 4:9 (2006).

[78] Edgar Schein, Inge Schneier, and Curtis H. Barker. Coercive pressure. (New York: Norton, 1961).

[79] Robert B. Cialdini, Rodney Bassett, and John T. Cacioppo. Low-ball procedure for producing compliance. Journal of Personality and Social Psychology, 36:5 (1978) 463-76.

person will be more likely to accede to a request if he or she previously has agreed to a smaller related request." In cases of low-
ball technique, they reassert that an individual's "compliance is
gained by not telling the person the whole story."

When applied to their content analysis of four white power
websites, Weatherby and Scroggins found both strategies were
employed as common recruiting techniques by inscribers to
"make [their] site's message appear less extreme." Examples included "links to sites such as the League of the South or Holocaust denial sites that appear scholarly, but in reality can be a
first step toward indoctrinating people with extremist beliefs."
Further, they assert that "any attempt to clean up a group's reputation, whether it has a .org address or a plea to be understood,
[should] be considered foot-in-the-door or low-ball technique"
(p. 19). In their study, Stormfront.org and the Imperial Klans of
America websites displayed the most examples of these contextual strategies. However, when we return to the earlier examples
of white power adaptations in cyberspace, it is clear to see foot-
in-the-door and low-ball methods being applied to the supremacist replicas of online culture. For instance, websites like the New
Saxon, which initially offer the promise of a new social network
but instead deliver a stream of racist ideology, practice a modern
form of foot-in-the-door technique that exploits a trusted cultural
institution of cyberspace. The Vanguard News Network and
Metapedia websites thrive on low-ball style content on their
pages that offer "news and information," but only supply the half
of the story that presents readers with a racist interpretation of
the facts.

In this research, we will see broad and refined applications of
these and other recruiting techniques. At the broad end, hate
sites incorporate many themes on their homepage that are aimed
to entice younger audiences, particularly those seeking an alternative community with which to identify. Simi and Futrell (2006)
noted how hate groups attract young adults who feel "disenfranchised" and "marginalized" in their own social environments,
and as such, turn to the Internet to find refuge in a web community that proclaims, "there's other people out there that think like

you."[80] Several studies have observed that it is often the "lonely, marginalized youth, seeking a sense of identity and belonging" who are the "most attractive targets for racists."[81] Hate websites tend to build upon this sense of welcoming in the outsider by constructing messages thematically-linked to one form of social identity or another; whether it be cultural, religious, political, patriotic, or something else, the underlying subtext is still black and white.

However, within the more refined recruiting bases (often the forums and downloadable contents of these sites) a narrower approach is evident in the framed messages of intolerance. These messages, posed as contemporary forum topics, are introduced by the hate website and its associated inscribers, and gradually accepted by new members. Whereas once these topics were overtly related to race, today's messages tactically overlap with mainstream concerns that affect the young generation in particular. Concerns like getting into college and high school gangs feed into more desirable racial themes like affirmative action and black gangs, respectively, which in turn, build upon the ideal white supremacist frames of black hatred and white unity.

But recent spikes in racist activity across American political culture have also allowed white power groups to broaden their field of recruitment and message strategy with young adults. Previously these goals had been limited to social outcast and fringe-based subcultures, but today organized hate groups are capitalizing on anti-government sentiment that is potentially delivering a more "mainstreamed" racist to their cause. According to the ADL, for instance, white power groups targeted the anti-tax

[80] Pete Simi and Robert Futrell. Cyberculture and the Endurance of White Power Activism. Journal of Political and Military Sociology, 34:1 (2006) 115:142.
[81] "Tactics for Recruiting Young People." Retrieved September 2, 2009, from
http://www.mediaawarness.ca/english/issues/online_hate/tactic_recr uit_
young.cfm

"Tea-Parties" of 2009 in order to cultivate an "organized grassroots White mass movement" amid all of the anti-President
Obama discourse.[82] This phenomenon is referred to as *transmove-
ment fluidity,* in which a youthful subculture or political movement
can "overlap with significant crossover between" a racist group's
agenda.[83] For white power groups, this overlap carries "important strategic implications for the development of alliances in the
movement," by conveniently incorporating other narratives of
social dissent. Later, this research will consider some of these current themes which tap into the disenfranchised identities of their
target audience, mainly youth-related frames of social rebellion
and uprising.

Returning to net generation and the popular culture of cyberspace, it is important to note that one need not necessarily
enter an organized white power website to encounter these kinds
of strategies of recruitment and messages of racial intolerance.
Certainly, major social networks and video-sharing websites like
Facebook and YouTube, respectively, have already been cited as
areas that have been infiltrated by white power ideologues and
racist organizations looking to preach and recruit. However,
what about the other cultural hangouts in cyberspace, particularly the worlds of online gaming and music?

Gardner (2000) asserted that the Internet "allows children to
travel daily…to a world where parental supervision is almost impossible and where a *Lord of the Flies* ethic rules."[84] Perhaps nowhere is this observation truer today than in the realm of live
interactive online gaming. Through headsets and remotes, kids

---

[82] "White Supremacists May Attempt to Co-Opt July 4 "Tea Parties"
To Promote Hateful Agenda." Retrieved on September 3, 2009, from
http://www.adl.org/PresRele/Extremism_72/5560_72.htm
[83] Betty A. Dobratz and Lisa K. Waldner. "In Search of Understanding
the White Power Movement." Journal of Political and Military Sociology, 34:1 (2006).
[84] Ralph Gardner, Jr. "Parenting: Is AOL worse than TV?" New York
Magazine (2000).

everywhere are entering fantasy worlds with intentions to kill – virtually of course. And while most game play is intended to be social, the level of violence matched by the competitiveness of the players can easily turn a friendly environment into a racist atmosphere. One 14-year-old gamer explains:

> Most social games are meant for friends to play together as opposed to "matchmaking" games or "deathmatches" commonly referred to as Multiplayer where gamers are hostile. These consist of gamers shouting racial slurs and sexual comments. Names, quotes, mottos and biographies can contain offensive information, as well as "screenshots" (in-game pictures) that convey racist themes. Video games and their wiring into the online world allow for the free flow of racist opinions and content that can easily be absorbed and then spread by the next recipient. (Liam Klein, personal communications, September 9, 2009).

In "Racism among the many foes online gamers must fight," Totilo (2005) chronicles the experiences of gamers from ages 7 to 23 who have been the recipients of such harassment.[85] One player, an African-American college student who identifies his race online noted how frequently he is verbally attacked by racists players with such comments as, "Jesus wasn't black, you stupid n-gger." Another father of a seven-year-old "prodigy" of the gaming world was shocked to discover how often the "n" word and other racial slurs were being cast at his son and other players. While there is no evidence of any forms of organized racism infiltrating the mainstream games, to date, the white supremacist world has caught on to the gaming market. In 2002, the National Alliance-run Resistance Records released "Ethnic Cleansing – the Game."[86] This neo-Nazi game that depicts a racial war being

---

[85] Stephen Totilo. "Racism Among the Many Foes Online Gamers Must Fight." Retrieved on August 28, 2009, from http://www.mtv.com/news/articles/1514305/20051121/index.jhtml (2005)
[86] "Games Extremists Play." Retrieved on September 1, 2009, from http://www.splcenter.org/ntel/intelreport/article.jsp?aid=124 (2002).

waged against all minorities can be downloaded on the Internet and played among friends. Other racial war-based games currently in the works include "Shoot the Blacks" and "Turner Diaries: the Game."

Like online gaming, the music culture of cyberspace is a direct conduit into the interests and activities of the net generation. Here, too, the white power movement has made serious inroads into their melodic digital environments via both mainstream and fringe-based websites. However, white power music was not born online. During the resurgence of white nationalism in the United States and Europe in the 1980s, neo-Nazi and Skinhead culture began to grow younger, angrier, and more expressive through loud music gatherings that would draw in thousands. Today, thousands have turned into millions online where white supremacist record labels like Resistance Records and Final Stand Records tap directly into an alarmingly large hate music market. Hate music is one of the leading commercial enterprises for white supremacists, but its revenues are worth much more than dollars and cents. The net generation and music go hand in hand in cyberspace where the concept of "mainstream" and "commercialism" have been redefined by controversial music-sharing sites such as Limewire. For the white power movement, their version of racist rock sounds very much like the metal-thrashing melodies that are popular with many predominantly white young males. But of course, their lyrics convey much more than angst. Cohen (2003) explains:

> The allure of the angry-sounding music often entices the loner teenager before he or she recognizes the significance of the lyrics. Sometimes the lyrics themselves are the draw. Teenagers who feel alienated by their peers are most susceptible to hate rock's message of solidarity and pride in the white race.[87]

---

[87] Adam Cohen. "White Power Music is an Effective Recruiting Tool." In White Supremacy Groups, (Farmington Hills, MI: Greenhaven Press, 2003).

Simi and Futrell's 2006 study noted how today's white power music-based sites offer not only "MP3 downloads, CDs, streaming radio and video" but also what they observe as "political lifestyle models of Aryan activism which viewers are encouraged to assimilate and reproduce" (p. 129). In addition to white power music websites, supremacist rock bands have also infiltrated mainstream bases like YouTube and Twitter with their songs, videos, and subculture, and have steadily built a young following there.

Ultimately, the music of racist rock, the sales of various paraphernalia like "videos, jewelry, and clothing," and the recent production of racial war interactive games, signal a disturbing trend upon two fronts. First, these are all examples of highly sophisticated foot-in-the-door techniques of recruitment. By fashioning familiar sounding music and violent video games, the white power movement is merely opening the door to the base of online youth culture. From there, the young browser can link deeper to another layer of racist subculture, one which they might have never considered entering before had they not been lured by that initial song or game.

On the second front, however, we are beginning to see the next phase of the online adaptation of the white power movement in their merchandising of all things "white power." The branding of hate symbols and trademarks onto stickers and jackets, as well as the sales of racist music suggest an overall culture which the white power movement is attempting to market online. The popular website aryanwear.com, for instance, sells traditional Nazi apparel that has been reproduced in more contemporary styles, as well as computer mouse pads, DVDs, sunglasses, and even pet wear that has all been branded in white nationalist emblems.[88] Today's hate organizations are clearly demonstrating a keen understanding of the connection between commerce and youth culture. One need only visit any American high school or college campus to see how overtly this generation expresses their

---

[88] Aryanwear. Retrieved on September 1, 2009, from http://aryanwear.com/

personality through styles, symbols, music, and tee-shirt slogans, all of which are considered extensions of self. For this reason, the white power movement has stepped up its commercial enterprises of youth culture in order to ultimately market the real product that these websites are selling – an all white identity.

Conclusion

There is no mystery behind why white power organizations, like many social movements, seek to recruit young minds into their cause. Their idealism and typically-rebellious inclinations make the younger generation a prime target for alternative-based organizations, especially those which stand for anti-establishment themes, i.e., anti-federal government or anti-cultural conformity. But recruitment of the net generation is of particular interest to the white power movements that have invested so much time and money in adapting to their cyber domain, because, in a very real way, these kids represent the next frontline of racists. As Stormfront.org founder, Don Black, explains:

> The Net itself is, as I have mentioned, an alternative news media…we feel that we are planting the seeds with these people which will grow and later may be the basis for a more viable political movement. These are people who frequently are in government or corporations, the military, or even the news media. These are people who are really important to us. I don't think we're going to have any kind of revolution strictly from the outside. (Nieli & Swain, 2003)

For the net generation, online culture is much more than just music downloading, interactive gaming, and instant messaging. It is their virtual "safe zone" for self-expression, social development, and even experimentation. It is a place to map out an identity. For the white power movement, on the other hand, online culture is also more than the sum of its applications and access points. It is a direct link to the next generation; a delivery system for receiving young, white social outcasts in search of an alternative community to call their own. The popular culture of cyberspace – the music, games, and social networks – provide the white power movement with nothing more than the necessary soundtrack, fantasy, and allure to entice today's young Internet-user. Once that door has been opened, the ultimate goal of course is to lead that prospective recruit from the cultural cross-sections of cyberspace into the core domain of the white power movement – the organizations' websites.

4. The Websites

When the global community entered the computerized information age, the doors to cyberspace were opened to anyone who could access and utilize the new medium. Through increased connectivity, preexisting forums of social and political expression found new homes in the virtual world where the concept of a community swiftly became a global sphere of unlimited communicative potential. Suddenly, everyone had a microphone on the world stage.

Organized hate speech, as a form of social-political expression, quickly emerged on the Internet through budding websites, discussion boards, chat rooms, and most recently, the blogosphere. The white power movement in particular moved to reestablish itself on the new platform, and over the last fifteen years it has steadily expounded its agenda in cyberspace. In fact, the very first white power website, Stormfront.org, was launched as early as 1995 and has since grown into one of the largest special interest communities online today. In this chapter, the first of three research sections, we will look at 26 select websites like Stormfront that have emerged, adapted, and under a newfound legitimacy, thrived on the World Wide Web.

From a global perspective, the number of organized hate sites currently active online exceeds 10,000 according to the Simon Wiesenthal Center, one of the leading watchdog organizations of extremist activity (2009).[89]

While 10,000 is no doubt a staggering number, especially when one considers the size of any given topic on the web, it should be understood in the greater context of a global media market, and one that includes not only the white power movement but also terrorist organizations, political groups from the

---

[89] Simon Wiesenthal Center (2009). Facebook, YouTube+: How Social Media Outlets Impact Digital Terrorism and Hate. Produced by the Simon Wiesenthal Center & Snider Social Action Institute.

radical right and left, as well as religious extremists now operating on almost every platform of the Internet. In its broadest conception, organized hate speech has truly become a modern pandemic phenomenon.

This branch of research, however, is primarily concerned with one central division among the 10,000 which, until now, we have broadly defined as the white power movement. In fact, as this chapter will illustrate in its presentation of 26 websites, the white power movement is hardly a centralized front but rather a complex social and political network in itself. As Swain and Nieli quickly discovered in their 2003 study, "Anyone who spends a few hours surfing the various white nationalists and white racialist websites on the Internet will discover just how vast the network of these organizations has become over the past few years." And yet, though it seems trivial to catalog the differences amongst racist sentiments – most of which are shared across the board anyway – there are notable variances within the network of white power ideology. Today, the leaders and inscribers of racist movements are usually classified into a few discernable categories: Neo-Nazis, White Nationalists (which include Racist Skinheads), as well as more focused fronts like anti-Semitic/Holocaust Denial groups, and the anti-Gay and anti-Hispanic organizations. Here, the research will introduce the entire sample under investigation by the identified movement with which these websites associate the content of their pages.

The selection of sites examined here, though intended for a more in-depth analysis, nonetheless was chosen to reflect a greater representational cross-section of white power activity on the Internet. As such, the three central criteria for selecting each site were its size, affiliation, and its representation of modern Internet trends. Not surprisingly, these three measures often complemented one another in the early investigation. That is to say the larger the website (the more frequented by online users), the more likely it was already associated with an active white power affiliate such as the Ku Klux Klan. Subsequently, those same websites with a broader following and a pre-established network often presented more complete and functional homepages representing today's most common cyber features such as convergent media links, social network forums, and evermore increasingly, academic research tools.

Table 4.1 – 26 Websites Under Investigation[90]

Websites	Primary Movement	Sample Traffic Ranking	Websites Linking In
American Renaissance	White Supremacist	2	649
Blood and Honour	Neo-Nazi Skinhead	13	74
Charles Darwin Research Institute	White Supremacist	23	63
Council of Conservative Citizens	White Nationalists Gay Hate	10	604
Creativity Alliance	White Supremacist	26	5
Final Solution 88	Anti-Semitic	18	43
God Hates Fags	Gay Hate	5	585
Hammerskin Nation	Racist Skinhead	17	35
Institute for Historical Review	Holocaust Denial	6	674
Jew Watch News	Anti-Semitic	9	421
Ku Klux Klan	Racist/Anti-Semitic	8	194
Metapedia	White Nationalist	3	32
National Alliance	Neo-Nazi	15	244
Nationalist Coalition	Neo-Nazi	19	22
National Socialist Movement	Neo-Nazi	12	122
New Saxon	White Supremacist	14	24

[90] Most Frequented White Power Websites. Data on traffic ranking provided by Alexa Web Information, June 30, 2009

Podblanc	White Supremacist	4	102
Stormfront	Racist/Anti-Semitic	1	1,286
Supreme White Alliance	Racist Skinhead	21	4
Vanguard News Network	Anti-Semitic	11	191
Vinlanders Social Club	Racist Skinhead	24	5
Volksfront	Neo-Nazi	20	16
White Aryan Resistance	Neo-Nazi	7	157
White Boy Society	Anti-Hispanic Racist	25	6
White Civil Rights	White Nationalist	16	103
Women for Aryan Unity	Neo-Nazi	22	2

Table 4.2 – Website Offerings

Websites	"Information" & Research Provider	Social Networking & Membership
American Renaissance	●	●
Blood and Honour		●
Charles Darwin Research Institute	●	
Council of Conservative Citizens	●	●
Creativity Alliance	●	●
Final Solution 88	●	
God Hates Fags	●	●
Hammerskin Nation		●
Institute for Historical Review	●	

Jew Watch News	•	•
Ku Klux Klan	•	•
Metapedia	•	•
National Alliance	•	•
Nationalist Coalition		
National Socialist Movement	•	•
New Saxon		•
Podblanc	•	•
Stormfront	•	•
Supreme White Alliance		•
Vanguard News Network	•	•
Vinlanders Social Club		•
Volksfront		•
White Aryan Resistance	•	•
White Boy Society		•
White Civil Rights	•	
Women for Aryan Unity		•

In a few cases that will be explored later in the study, websites were chosen strictly because they represented a significant growing demographic such as the Women for Aryan Unity website, a neo-Nazi female assembly associated with the National Alliance and currently on the rise.

Collectively the sample presented here represents a stunning transformation from a movement that once could be characterized at best as an underground subculture of extremists into the list you see in table 4.1: an overt and vibrant community. How

yesterday's extremist elements of society have transitioned, or
perhaps more aptly, *adapted* into this new generation can only be
understood by ultimately going directly to the source – the websites themselves – and examining their pages from the initial Internet-user's point of view.

The Neo-Nazis

As a recurring news story, hate activity in the media has often been captured in images of the neo-Nazi banner marching
through the streets of Small Town, USA. Depending upon one's
perspective, the sudden resurfacing of a neo-Nazi rally behind
the banner of swastikas can appear as a frightening reprisal of
1930s Germany, or an angry mob of teenagers in need of attention. While there is certainly no façade to the threat of this nos-
talgic movement, the transmission of its public message had been
largely deflated throughout the 1980s and 90s and confined to
underground books, underground music, and flyers that led to
underground meetings. That is until its most recent efforts to resurface in the online community.

It is appropriate to begin this exploration through the fringes
of cyberspace with one of the most identified hate factions in
modern history, the neo-Nazis, whose agenda and message of
intolerance are among the most recognized and extreme, and
therefore, familiar in society. In some ways, the neo-Nazi front
presents to us one end of a spectrum of transparency in the white
power arena. Here, we might expect to see the Internet used as a
medium by the neo-Nazis in the same way that radios and billboards were once employed by Hitler's Nazi Party, recalling
their use of newspapers to present the Jews as sinister cartoons
plotting in the shadows, or as the vermin and rats of German
society. While their underlying message is still very much the
same, the medium and the generation it attempts to reach have
changed, and so, too, have the leading neo-Nazi websites in their
strategy to reflect a modern and above-ground approach to Hitler's cherished ideals.

The Southern Poverty Law Center, another national leader in the fight against intolerance, both legally and on the educational front, has defined the neo-Nazi agenda by its shared "hatred for Jews and a love for Adolf Hitler and Nazi Germany."[91] This watchdog group notes further that, "While [neo-Nazis] also hate other minorities, homosexuals and even sometimes Christians, they perceive "the Jew" as their cardinal enemy, and trace social problems to a Jewish conspiracy that supposedly controls governments, financial institutions and the media." This element of "control" and a perceived "conspiracy" plays a major role in the neo-Nazi discourse. However, in recent years the neo-Nazis in the United States have expanded their mission beyond anti-Semitism to include a newly targeted Hispanic population. That exclusive American cause centers largely on the growing immigration debate which lends the neo-Nazi agenda a familiar theme of the "outsider" threatening the white establishment from within. Leading the pack in terms of notoriety and reach is the *National Socialist Movement* (NSM), the largest neo-Nazi group in the United States.

In the real fabric of American society, and in particular, the Midwest, NSM members are high on the radar of most law enforcement agencies aware of their growing presence around local political issues and the occasional college campus. When active, they are hard to miss donned in swastika-patched armbands, unranked uniforms, and even at times standing behind actual shields like pseudo-soldiers. In cyberspace, however, their presence lies unshielded from anyone who stumbles upon the URL, nsm88.org. Of course, to most everyday citizens the prospect of stumbling into the website of one of the leading neo-Nazi groups in the United States would be like intentionally driving your car into the bad part of town. However, with over 120 websites currently linking into the nsm88.org domain including Wikipedia, Google, and Yahoo, that prospect becomes less an act of deliberate consciousness and more of a foolish wrong turn.

---

[91] "Active U.S. Hate Groups in 2008: Neo-Nazi." Retrieved June 28, 2009, from http://www.splcenter.org/intel/map/type.jsp?DT=9.

As this research will show, this can be especially true for the high school or college student clicking their way through an online academic search.

Returning to the earlier spectrum of transparency, the homepage of the NSM website could not likely be confused for anything other than a neo-Nazi gathering place. Like the news broadcasts they occasional spotlight, the NSM page is swathed with images from its rallies, traditional swastikas, and currently, a cartoon depicting a Star of David-shaped intersection leading directly to the White House – again, the theme of Jewish control and conspiracy are insinuated upfront.[92] The name Hitler appears several times on the homepage and the site's URL containing the number 88 is a common neo-Nazi reference to "Heil Hitler" from the numeric correlation to the eighth letter of the alphabet: HH. These various numeric symbols are common to white supremacist communications, and along with exploited images like the Celtic cross allow groups like the NSM to brand and market their agendas online into tee-shirts, music labels, and badges of honor.

While an initial scan of the NSM homepage draws upon familiar Nazi imagery and an overall militant feel, a snapshot of this website's features reveals much more about its modernized strategy aimed at attracting a newer generation of visitors to its cause. Like all the websites studied in this sample, nsm88.org undeniably fits into the criteria of representative of contemporary Internet trends. From video and audio convergence to mainstream links like YouTube, fully-functioning community blogs to racially biased news stories, the NSM site demonstrates sophistication in its ability to package their initial message into the new medium. The homepage presented mostly in red, white, and blue and displaying a picture of a bald eagle, is at first glance an American political page that provides both community and information to its visitors. That basic equation – race and country

---

[92] The National Socialist Movement. Retrieved June 20, 2009, from http://www.nsm88.org/

– will repeat several times throughout this study, albeit to different degrees and through a variety of veiled messages.

Another National Socialist Movement creation, the *New Saxon* website, offers online visitors a similar agenda on its homepage. It advocates for "the rights of white people, preservation of European culture and heritage, reform of illegal immigration policies" and other white power-based standards that are expressed above the swastika-draped American flag.[93] However, the New Saxon website presents a strategically modified approach to the cause as a strict social networking site that appears to broaden its base slightly beyond the traditional anti-Semitic/neo-Nazi movement to attract more white supremacist audiences as well. The New Saxon calls itself "An online community for whites by whites" primarily aimed at bringing people of common interests together. According to the Anti-Defamation League (ADL), the New Saxon is "not as feature friendly as mainstream sites, [but] it remains popular with the white supremacists and provides a way for the NSM to recruit new members."[94]

In addition to the National Socialist Movement, other major websites associated with the neo-Nazi banner in this sample include the *Nationalist Coalition, National Alliance* and *Women for Aryan Unity, Final Solution 88, Volksfront* and the *White Aryan Resistance* (WAR). Like the NSM and New Saxon sites, all of these neo-Nazi communities demonstrate a high level of technical savvy and sophistication on their homepages. The multimedia picture galleries of Volksfront.org, for instance, carefully hide the faces of members behind enlarged pixels nevertheless emphasizing the close-knit community itself, while the Nationalist Coalition web-

---

[93] The New Saxon. "An online community for whites by whites." Retrieved June 20, 2009, from http://newsaxon.org/

[94] The National Socialist Movement. "Tactics." Retrieved on June 22, 2009, from http://www.adl.org/
Learn/Ext_US/nsm/tactics.asp?LEARN_Cat
=Extremism&LEARN_SubCat=Extreism_in_America&xpicked=3
&item=nsm

site acts much like an intersecting superhighway with dozens of links to other hate group websites and mainstream content on YouTube. The WAR homepage launched under the attractive moniker resist.com provides video games and cartoons for an apparently younger target audience. However, with their forums on International Jewry, virtual leaflets on anti-Israel and Holocaust Denial campaigns, and "About Us" statements that speak to Aryan ideals, the underlying neo-Nazi tirade still scratches fairly close to the surface on most of these websites.

White Nationalists

If the neo-Nazis are among the more identifiable and discernable hate groups in cyberspace, then only a thin gray line separates them from the racist skinheads, part of the white nationalist clan. In an ideological sense, the skinhead movement is the most transparent of the white nationalists in terms of an expressed racist agenda. The Southern Poverty Law Center's (SPLC) definition of white nationalism as a whole includes those groups mainly "focusing on the alleged inferiority of nonwhites."[95] For our purposes, however, white nationalists like the skinheads include those groups whose websites convey a predominantly racist mission, especially toward people of color, whether in the name of nationalism, religion, science, or politics. This particular segment of the vast white power movement is by far the most expansive, and therefore, represented in this sample beginning with the skinheads.

Sometimes confused with the neo-Nazis, racists skinheads are seen as a particularly violent element of white nationalism. Many skinhead groups are affiliated with prison gangs exclusively, while others can be seen demonstrating out in the open on perceived matters of race such as immigration and civil rights, which they ardently oppose. Among their ranks, the *Hammerskin Nation, Blood and Honour, Supreme White Alliance*, and *Vinlanders Social*

---

[95] White Nationalism. Retrieved on June 20, 2009, from http://www.splcenter.org/intel/intelreport/article.jsp?aid=863 (2007)

Club have each launched websites with notably similar content
and even a few shared links between them, which in itself is significant considering that many of the same groups have been at
odds with one another in the past. Online, however, these four
skinhead communities share memberships and qualities of having an edgier homepage marked by the symbols and fashion of
their hardcore society. The skinhead subculture, which has seen
strong resurgences over the last 20 years, is very much an international movement with roots in Great Britain that now span
over much of Europe and North America. That movement is
often viewed as appealing to younger outcasts, males in particular, who are attracted to a scene entrenched in social rebellion,
underground music gatherings, and having a gang-like brotherhood. These cultural elements were quite present on the homepages of their websites. In addition to tattoos and army boots,
however, the sites investigated here show notable interest in current affairs and politics as they relate to matters of race. For instance, the Supreme White Alliance website opens with a video
link documenting the "deception" of U.S. President Barack
Obama.[96] In the next section, the analysis will highlight further
how the nomination of the first black American President has
renewed a fiery hatred of African-Americans among the white
nationalist circles.

Perhaps just as recognizable as the skinheads have become in
symbolizing traditional hate speech across the globe, the *Ku Klux
Klan* (KKK) are potentially the most identifiable white supremacist movement across the United States. According to the Anti-
Defamation League, the KKK remains one of the single largest
hate groups in the country with the greatest number of national
and local organizations. The ADL defines the KKK as a "racist,
anti-Semitic movement with a commitment to extreme violence
to achieve its goals of racial segregation and white supremacy."[97]

---

[96] Supreme White Alliance. Retrieved June 20, 2009, from
http://swa43.com/drupal/
[97] "About the KKK." Retrieved June 21, 2009, from
http://www.adl.org/

Forming its ranks not long after the end of the Civil War, the
KKK is certainly one of the oldest active hate organizations in
the world today, well-known for their bigoted platform and the
white hoods they hide behind. In recent years, the Internet has
provided a new form of anonymity for the KKK where they can
rebuild a racist political network which had lost much of it membership and clout in the last 40 years. In fact, according to Samoriski (2002), this rebuilding process has been one of the major
functions of the cyber movement for the white nationalist stage at
large:

> Organizations such as the Ku Klux Klan (KKK), traditionally
> involved in real world demonstrations, parades, and leafleting
> to gain publicity, have found the ease and low cost of Internet
> publishing ideally suited for their public relations needs. Such
> organizations are able to create and maintain Web sites to
> communicate with existing members and reach new ones
> much more cheaply than they can produce and distribute a
> newsletter or magazine. Hate groups are also able to link to
> other sites, thereby creating a hate network on the Internet.[98]

These observations hold true for the current KKK website
which is updated constantly. The nationwide hate group has, in
effect, built a virtual headquarters in cyberspace linking all of its
smaller chapters while connecting them to other leading white
nationalist sites such as Stormfront, demonstrating how the Internet has grown the cause beyond the grassroots level. According to the ADL, this strategy has worked well for the KKK: "After a period of relative quiet, Ku Klux Klan activity has spiked
noticeably upwards in 2006, as Klan groups have attempted to
exploit fears in America over gay marriage, perceived "assaults"
on Christianity, crime and especially immigration." Those same
issues of gay marriage, the encroachment on white Christian val-

---

learn/ext_us/kkk/default.asp?LEARN_Cat=Extremism&LEARN_Su
bCat=Extremism_in_America&xpicked=4&item=kkk
[98] Jan Samoriski. Issues in Cyberspace: Communication, Technology,
Law, and Society on the Internet Frontier. (Boston, MA: Allyn and
Bacon, 2002) 251.

ues, crime in the black community, and the immigration debate, are all present in the white nationalist circle of websites and have become the working tools of their trade. While there is a place for these matters to be debated in political and social arenas such as the blogosphere, websites like Stormfront have been able to capitalize on these social-political dilemmas by infusing their own heavy dose of racist sentiment into the discussion.

As illustrated earlier in Table 5.1, it is clear that *Stormfront* is by far the largest, most frequented URL among all the hate websites on the web. A predominantly white nationalist site, Stormfront demonstrates one of the most elaborate and complete transitions of hate speech into the online platform. It has been described by the ADL as a "veritable supermarket of online hate, stocking its shelves with many forms of anti-Semitism and racism" including forums ranging on subjects of parenting to teens, classified ads to home and gardening, and an alarmingly interactive chat community.[99] Stormfront is perhaps the most advanced of the hate group websites because it has been around for 15 years and has evolved steadily with the changing times. Its founder, Don Black, not surprisingly was a longtime student of the white power movement and a former member of the KKK which he helped revitalize with David Duke before turning his attention to the Internet. Today, Stormfront reportedly receives "tens of thousands of visitors each month," and for many, is only the first stop en route to its more extremist links among the "outer fringes of neo-Nazi and white militia groups."[100] Visually, Stormfront is structured like a multipurpose community database (i.e., Craigslist), but internally it delivers a virtual hornet's nest of social intolerance to its community of visitors.

Not all of the white nationalist websites, however, use social forums like those of Stormfront to invoke the sentiments of intol-

---

[99] Don Black: White Pride World Wide. Retrieved on June 19, 2009, from http://www.adl.org/poisoning_web/black.asp
[100] Carol M. Swain and Russ Nieli. Contemporary Voices of White Nationalism in America.
(Cambridge, UK: Cambridge University Press, 2003) 253.

erance. Some in this sample turn to the pages of history, politics, and science in attempts to "educate" their readers on race. The *American Renaissance* website, for instance, posts content that professes to expose a corrupt side of Martin Luther King, Jr., while the *Charles Darwin Research Institute* site uses selective science and history to make the case for a white supremacy based upon the laws of evolution. The *Creativity Alliance* website appears to take that message to the next level by incorporating religion with evolution. This site is crowned by the image of a halo surrounded by a DNA double-helix and resting atop the letter W (for white). It proclaims to be a "religious creed" based on the scientific work of Charles Darwin, and thus delivers a faith-based blend of education and intolerance. The Creative Alliance received national attention from the notoriety of its founder, Matthew Hale, who has appeared in several TV newscasts and magazine interviews to promote his brand of spiritual white supremacy. Hale, who was denied his law license by the Illinois Bar Association, went on instead to become "Pontifex Maximus" of the World Church of the Creator at age 25. Incidentally, Pontifex maximus started his website in 2005 out of his home office, the second floor study of his father's house in East Peoria, Illinois.[101] Both the Creativity movement and Hale's site, however, have built a worldwide membership.

On the theoretical spectrum of transparency, the general appearance of websites like Stormfront or the Creativity Alliance, while promoting white supremacist themes, do not immediately stand out as typical bases for hate. It is within this area of the white nationalist family that those political, religious and educational outlets of cyberspace begin to payoff in their ability to promote racial war while maintaining the appearance of a typical online community. David Duke's *White Civil Rights* website, for example, includes mainstream national news stories on its homepage aimed at painting a consistent picture of a menacing Black community. Other supremacist sites like *Podblanc,*

---

[101] Angie Cannon and Warren Cohen. "The Church of the Almighty White Man." U.S. News & World Report, 127:3 (1999, July 19)

Metapedia, and the *Council of Conservative Citizens* appear to transcend the world of hate in attempts to reach a more mainstream audience and status. The first two of these sites, Podblanc and Metapedia were founded in the last three years, and have each been carefully documented by the SPLC as next generation hate websites.

Podblanc, "a video-sharing website that's fast becoming an online institution for the white nationalist movement...[is] modeled after YouTube," the Center reports.[102] In cyberspace, convergent media sites, particularly video-sharing hubs, have become the latest form of online social expression for younger net-savvy communities. Podblanc taps into this youth-driven platform with over 1,000 channels, many of which exploit race humor and amateur comedy sketches. However, other postings, such as those documented by the SPLC, depict "montages of skinheads...punching, kicking and stomping orthodox Jews and nonwhites. The victims appear to be selected at random as they ride subways and walk down public streets."

Like Podblanc, Metapedia is the alternative form of another modern cyber phenomenon, Wikipedia. This white nationalist website is designed to offer Internet-users an educational encyclopedia on tens of thousands of subjects, providing of course, a racial spin on their explanations. Metapedia, which looks and behaves just like Wikipedia, is also offered in ten different languages each rapidly growing in popularity. It is not a self-ascribed white nationalist movement like other websites, but rather presents itself as an "alternative encyclopedia" updated daily. The SPLC identifies Metapedia as a clear indication that white power communities are attempting to reach mainstream academics, but reaffirms that while their scholarly "subjects sound familiar...their definitions don't."[103]

---

[102] "Behind the Gunfire. Alleged Murderer Inspired By Podblanc Website." Retrieved on June 23, 2009 from
http://www.splcenter.org/intel/intelreport/article.jsp?aid=1065
[103] "Aryan Encyclopedia Takes Off." Retrieved on June 20, 2009, from
http://www.splcenter.org/intel/intelreport/article.jsp?aid=863 (2007)

The final website in this section is probably the most likely to dispute its place on this list. The Council of Conservative Citizens (CCC) establishes its organization's principles over its website as a pledge to support "American civilization, liberty, justice, and national safety," but its content and history tell a different story.[104] On its face, the CCC appears to be a respectable right-wing representative with strong connections to politics, but its initiatives are designed for a United States of America which they define as solely "Christian" and "European." In 2004, Beirich and Moser studied some of the positions disseminated by this semi-mainstream political website. They concluded that the CCC was, in fact, "a hate group that routinely denigrated blacks as 'genetically inferior,' complained about 'Jewish power brokers,' called homosexuals 'perverted sodomites,' and accused immigrants of turning America into a 'slimy brown mass of glop.'"[105] The CCC website represents perhaps one of the most significant cases in the entire sample because of its established connections to southern GOP political figures like Senator Trent Lott and Governor Haley Barbour of Mississippi, but more so because of its successful masking of racist sentiments behind the discourse of professed conservative values. The website reports heavily on "nonwhite" criminal activity, though it is not a news website, and provides feature articles dedicated almost exclusively to outlining racial differences within American society, yet consistently only finds fault with African-Americans, Jews, Hispanics and gay citizens. The CCC website further uses recurring themes of national safety and patriotism to bolster its content regarding the threat to white, Christian society. In fact, this fear-tactic strategy is one of the oldest hallmarks of white nationalism and will be examined further.

---

[104] The Council of Conservative Citizens. Retrieved on June 22, 2009, from http://cofcc.org/

[105] Heidi Beirich and Ben Moser. "Communing with the Council." Retrieved June 20, 2009 from http://www.splcenter.org/intel/intelreport/article.jsp?aid=487 (2004)

Targeted Fronts

One of the primary reasons that the World Wide Web has blossomed into such a vast public sphere is that it became an immediate and ideal outlet for special interest groups to advocate their causes and communities worldwide. It was not long ago when people marveled at the speed with which the web had established homepages for virtually everything. Today, the phenomenon of burgeoning online communities is already commonplace, as the general public sphere of the Internet seemed to explode overnight into a million segments. The white power movement has also fragmented off from the elitist and popular stages of development into what Rodman (2008) called the specialized media stage, in which genres inevitably "break up into segments for audience members with diverse and specialized interests."[106] While most of the targeted minorities in this section are already central enemies for white power group websites like the Nationalist Coalition, this research sought to examine a few specialized websites with a strategically directed brand of hate speech.

Beginning with the most recurrent target in cyberspace, the Jewish community, the anti-Semitic movement is a fully developed specialized platform, even outside of general white nationalist and neo-Nazi circles. Among the websites examined here, the *Institute for Historical Review* (IHR) represents one of several Holocaust Denial organizations operating today, followed by *Jewwatch*, an online library of anti-Semitic content, and lastly, the *Vanguard News Network* which is dedicated to providing feature articles supporting the claim of a growing Jewish conspiracy. One of the values in researching specialized websites is that they tend to put the strategies of localized hate speech, such as anti-Semitism, under a microscope.

The Institute for Historical Review, for instance, funnels "scholarly" writings and analysis into an area of Holocaust study

---

[106] George Rodman. Mass Media in a Changing World: History, Industry, Controversy. (New York: McGraw-Hill, 2008) 141.

that was really created by anti-semitic organizations. According to the ADL, the IHR which was founded in 1978 by Willis Carto, strives to present its research at major international conferences and in respected journals, but has not succeeded in doing so since 2002.[107] This, of course, raises the question: Why would anyone pursue the scholarship of refuting the mass genocide of the Holocaust? The IHR website is a further indication of their movement's desire to secure a legitimate field from which to circulate anti-Semitic materials, and they believe that they have found it as a "historical resource" provider. Both the Jewwatch and Vanguard News Network websites also appear to mimic media designs in the mainstream by following familiar encyclopedic and informational formats. Among the subjects covered by the Jewwatch.com database are: Jewish Conspirators, Killers, Power Lords, Jewish Terrorists, and Jewish Mind Control Mechanisms. The Vanguard News Network offers news stories aimed at framing the Jewish people as the cause for the global economic crisis, Wall Street scandals, unpopular White House decisions, foreign conflicts of war, and the lists go on.

Like anti-Semitism, the racial front against Hispanic-Americans has also been surging at an alarming rate over the last ten years in connection with powerful anti-immigration sentiment. On the issue of immigration, this research is not concerned with the politics of the matter and for this reason several potential websites pre-examined here were not incorporated into the study because they were found to be strictly issue-oriented. However, anti-Hispanic hate speech is nevertheless rampant among white power circles. Every group from neo-Nazis to skinheads to the Ku Klux Klan has turned heavy attention to the Hispanic community, which is often highlighted within these sites by their presumed nationality such as Mexican or Puerto Rican. Some websites have become so consumed with their agendas of anti-Hispanic rhetoric that their pages have moved from the popular stage into a specialized function of hate mongering. One such

---

[107] Institute for Historical Review: Outlet for Denial Propaganda. Retrieved on June 21, 2009, from http://www.adl.org/holocaust/ihr.asp

site is the *White Boy Society*. A white supremacist biker group, the White Boy Society website offers cartoons, merchandise, and forums dedicated to Hispanic stereotypes and their perceived threat and inferiority in American culture. The website also takes a radical stance on immigration in its "Invasion USA" section that provides statistics on illegal aliens positioned next to an array of featured AK assault rifles and the advertisement "help save the country."[108]

Finally, the world of gay hatred has been overlooked by mainstream scrutiny for years despite the rising tide of aggressive and violent homophobic rhetoric in the media. To an extent, this is because stances taken against the gay and lesbian communities are still widely accepted in the conservative and religious circles and their views are often echoed in the news. As the social, cultural, and legal debate over civil issues such as gay marriage play out in the American courts of law and public opinion, an undeniably hateful strain of the anti-gay movement has forged an uglier face in cyberspace. One of the leading examples of this can be found at the URL *Godhatesfags.com*, the website of the Westboro Baptist Church (WBC).

The WBC first came into the national spotlight in 1998 when behind their church leader Fred Phelps, members picketed outside the funeral of Matthew Shepherd, the teenager from Laramie, Wyoming who was beaten to death because he was a homosexual. The signs they held back then very much reflected the same principles which can be found on their small, but growing website. Among the gallery of signs an Internet-user will immediately encounter when visiting the site are those that declare "God Hates Fags," "You're Going to Hell," "Fag Sin," "Fags Doom Nations," "God is America's Enemy" and "Jews Killed Jesus."[109] Like the website's founder, the blogs and forums it shares are framed by biblical justifications and reasoning, but the

---

[108] White Boy Society. Retrieved on June 20, 2009, from http://localwhiteboy.com/home.php
[109] God Hates Fags. Retrieved on June 20, 2009, from http://www.godhatesfags.com/.

"God Hates Fags" site is anything but ethical in its reviling and hatred of gays, Jews and many supporters, like President Obama, whom it frequently calls the "anti-Christ." Fred Phelps himself was disbarred by the Kansas Supreme Court in 1979 for making blatantly false accusations against a defendant and showing "little regard for the ethics of his profession."[110] His "church" has since been extremely vocal in their voicing of anti-Government senti- ment as well, most recently picketing outside the funerals of fallen Iraq and Afghanistan war soldiers with placards that read, "Thank God for Dead Soldiers."[111] The SPLC includes the Kan- sas-based Westboro Baptist Church high among its annual list of 946 active hate groups operating inside the United States today, while the ADL asserts that the WBC website is specifically "de- signed to inflame the passion of viewers."[112] With over 840 web- sites currently linking into godhatefags.com including Twitter, MySpace, Wikipedia, and Stormfront, the Westboro Baptist Church homepage is likely to do just that.

Sample Overview

From the initial overview, a few observations can be drawn about the sample of 26 websites as a whole. First, there appears to be a shared understanding among these established organiza- tions that, within cyberspace, the medium is just as important as the message it serves. Before the Internet age, most of these same

---

[110] "Fred Phelps Disbarred." Retrieved September 19, 2009, from http://www.adl.org/learn/ext_us/WBC/disbarred.asp?LEARN_Cat= Extremism&LEARN_SubCat=Extremism_in_America&xpicked=3 &item=WBC
[111] "Pickets inspire legislation and legal action." Retrieved on Septem- ber 19, 2009, from http://www.adl.org/learn/ext_us/WBC/ legislation.asp?LEARN_Cat=Extremism&LEARN_SubCat= Extremism_in_America&xpicked=3&item=WBC
[112] "Westboro Baptist Church: A publicity hungry-group." Retrieved on June 20, 2009, from http://www.adl.org/learn/ext_us/WBC/ publicity.asp?LEARN_Cat=Extremism&LEARN_SubCat= Extremism_in_America&xpicked=3&item=WBC

fringe elements had been disseminating their rhetoric through flyers and faxes and upon signs carried at the occasional staged rally. The homepage revolution suggests that the leaders of these movements have collectively sought to design virtual spaces that could become interactive communities. This is a significant change, because the new online message of white power that grows out of public forums, discussion boards, and chat rooms, essentially reverses the prior strategy of communicating the cause to anyone who would listen. In the anonymous public sphere of cyberspace, social movements of all kinds have discovered their ability to grow their causes from the inside, out.

The second observation about the sample overview concerns hate speech's changing position in the media courtesy of the World Wide Web. The focus on transparency, in particular, is really a consideration in a website's mainstream potential. While a few websites like Blood and Honour conveyed more traditional imagery via swastikas and other racist symbols, the majority of this sample reflects the white power message packaged behind more contemporary themes of politics, or education, or patriotism. Another factor in the development of white power websites is the loose standards of media in cyberspace. On the Internet, the concept of the mainstream media is stretched beyond standards that are instilled on television, where civil laws, morality, and social norms are seen to still prevail. Therefore, the white power movement instantly arrives at a more level playing field in cyberspace among the other political, educational and religious web communities. However, simply having a homepage and instant access to the public is not enough to establish solid ground on the web. You need a following. Luckily, for the white power movement, the population of racists and anti-Semites had been well-established around the world long before Stormfront.org was first launched in 1995. Since then, the numbers speak for themselves.

Hate Online: Size and Significance

The idea of size in cyberspace is significantly harder to comprehend than other mass media measurement tools such as the television rating system or motion picture sales. The Institute for Historical Review (Holocaust Denial) website, for instance, only receives an average .0005% of the world's Internet audience over a three month period, according to leading website information tool, Alexa.com.[113] In fact, when put into the proper perspective, that global share is quite significant. The Alexa web information database ranked IHR as the 261,155th most visited website, a number that only begins to resonate when measured against the estimated 180 million websites currently operating in cyberspace today. Within the more focused scale of special interest group sites, the size of the white power base is even more astounding.

If we begin by considering the largest and most frequented websites on the web such as Google, consistently ranked #1, Wikipedia (#7), MySpace (#11), and BBC (#43), we can branch out into more relevant subcategories of special interest groups where information studies specialists often consider the community in context. In this case, the community in context is the world of organized race, nationality, ethnic, and sexual orientation interest groups, or for our broader purposes, identity-based websites. When white supremacist sites are included in that definition as they aim to be, the significance of their place in cyberspace begins to take shape.

In the Table 4.3 and Figure 4.1, some of the world's leading identity-based organizations are measured against the most frequented white power websites in this sample with regard to average traffic rank and global Internet use. Even in the company of some of the most influential advocates for civil rights and social equality standards, the significance of the sample becomes self-evident. While not every website in this sample is as large as Stormfront, most sites like Metapedia and American Renaissance

---

[113] Alexa Web Information. "Institute for Historical Review." Retrieved on June 28, 2009 from http://alexa.com/siteinfo/ihr.org

are within range or even larger than competing voices like The Human Rights Campaign, NAACP, or even the Anti-Defamation League that works specifically against the rising tide of hate on the Internet. Theirs, however, may be a losing battle as long as hate websites continue to pursue a competitive strategy of bridging and building community memberships from the level of interconnectivity that only the Internet provides.

Table 4.3 – Special Interest Groups in Cyberspace

Organization and Website (Sites listed by average web traffic)	Traffic Ranking[114]
Stormfront (Stormfront.org)	#13,910
American Renaissance (Amren.com)	#72,930
Anti-Defamation League (ADL.org)	#78,176
Metapedia (Metapedia.org)	#81,158
Human Rights Campaign (HRC.org)	#99,080
Gay & Lesbian Alliance Against Defamation (GLAAD.org)	#171,939
National Organization for Women (NOW.org)	#189,268
National Association for the Advancement of Colored People (NAACP.org)	#265,066
National Council of La Raza (NCLR.org)	#309,724

---

[114] Website data provided by Alexa.org in June, 2009. Stormfront is ranked highest on this list that runs from the most to least frequented sites in this particular sample of special interest groups. In the broader overview of online web activity, Google is consistently ranked # 1.

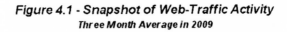

Figure 4.1 - Snapshot of Web-Traffic Activity
Three Month Average in 2009

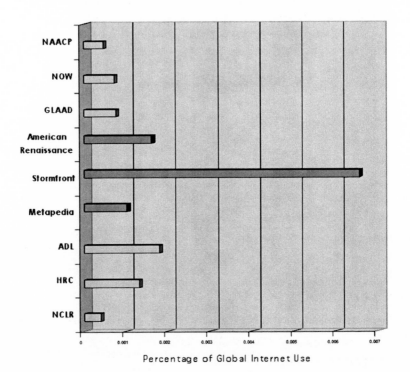

Percentage of Global Internet Use

Ultimately, size in cyberspace is multidimensional when one considers network links and the interconnectedness of an entire community. A visitor to the relatively benign-sounding Vinlanders Social Club, for instance, can link directly to the White Boy Society website, and from there move onto the Supreme White Alliance or Blood and Honour homepages, and dozens more interconnected to them, quickly demonstrating how the whole is greater than the sum of its parts in a highly active web community such as this.

Conclusion

Returning to the example of the Institute for Historical Review, interconnectivity in cyberspace is also a powerful concept because the door swings both ways. Just as the IHR page includes links to other Holocaust Denial websites that continuously branch out into the anti-semitic community, there are currently 674 documented sites that link directly back into the IHR homepage. And among them, you guessed it: Google, Wikipedia, MySpace, and BBC. In this way, the IHR website is a prime example of the informational laundering capacity of cyberspace which feeds off of the direct interconnectivity and the borrowed legitimacy of mainstream domains like BBC and Wikipedia. As one continues to connect the dots further, they soon find themselves deeply emerged inside the much larger white power community of websites.

The white power community in cyberspace is well-represented in this sample of 26 of the leading hate websites. It is clear to see that this collection of .coms and .orgs symbolizes a growing online movement that is diverse in focus and affiliation, but also integrated in community, style, and strategy. While the leaders and organizers of toxic subcultures like neo-Nazism and the Ku Klux Klan might have different ideas about who the primary enemy of the white society may be, the following findings will show that the spoken language of hate is largely universal among these bigoted societies. The messages they create tend to flow along parallel lines and lead toward similar ends, mainly the call-to-action against all the "nonwhite oppressors." This and other converging themes, like religious conspiracies and racial differences, are ultimately what really tie the white power community together. The Internet has simply packaged and qualified such sentiments, and delivered them to the masses.

5. Constructing the Racist Belief System

From the onset, this research has moved along on an outward trajectory through cyberspace. What began as an exploration of hate speech in the real world, cautiously ventured into the vast infrastructures of the World Wide Web. Through unguarded territories we set off to examine the furthest fringes of the Internet, traveling along mainstream and interconnected channels of search engines, news, and information websites. Our digital journey then passed through the cultural spheres of social networking and video-sharing websites where we found the white power movement had already established inroads to the net generation. Beyond these mainstream domains, we explored the quasi-cultural gathering places of white power music, gaming, and blogs where a distinguishable line between bigotry, entertainment, and debate had been distorted by the sound of hate rock and the bent logic of racially-charged politics. Suddenly, we reached our final and present destination, the white power movement websites. From the initial overview, the 26 representational sites offered a telling cross-section of what modernized hate speech looks like today. Now, we will shift our focus and trajectory inward to examine the features, strategies, and messages that these leading voices of hate have created within their web communities.

In many ways, this entire investigative design has been a process of peeling back layers; first, the outer layers of cyberspace, and now, the inner layer of the white power movement website. Keeping the Internet-user in mind, this final phase of the investigation begins at that initial point of entry for every website, the homepage. From here, the dissection process really begins as we employ methods like frame analysis (Goffman, 1974)[115] to pinpoint a clearer understanding, and perhaps, an

---

[115] Erving Goffman. Frame analysis: An Essay on the Organizational of Experience. (London: Harper and Row, 1974).

underlying truth about the nature of racism today as broadcast in its measurable online form. Like any contextual analysis, a few principal questions should guide our way as we consider these 26 websites collectively.

First, as objective visitors, we ask ourselves what common features stand out in these websites that capture the immediate attention and interest of an Internet-user. What apparent similarities in the presentations of their homepage can be quantified as a collective approach? We recall that Borrowman (1999) defined "techno-ethos" as the "credibility or authority that is constructed online in the programming proficiency demonstrated in a flashy web site."[116] Did these 26 websites demonstrate that kind of necessary flash and proficiency on their homepages?

Secondly, we should consider those qualitative commonalities of the content found in various features like news forums and mission statements. What set of facts and/or positions do they consistently convey? This is an important area to consider because it encourages the information studies and media scholar to identify current white power messages that exist on the fringe of cyberspace, from which they can later track their potential and subsequent penetrations into the mainstream venues of political and cultural discourse.

Thirdly, we should also identify how these facts and positions are delivered – their message formation. This area of the investigation speaks directly to those refined strategies of recruitment within these sites that were examined earlier, such as foot-in-the-door technique. In addition, rhetorical concepts such as *binary discourse* also play a major role in building an understanding about the way that the white power movement transforms an overt message of "racial war" into a nuanced expression of acceptable intolerance.

Finally, as a special extension to message formation within the white power domain, we focus on uncovering the codewords of hate speech at their true origin. Within the forums and con-

---

[116] Shane Borrowman. "Critical Surfing: Holocaust Deniability and Credibility on the Web." College Teaching, 47:2, (1999) 44-54.

fines of white power culture, this research can unearth the lexicon of terms that we normally do not recognize as the rally cries and secret handshakes of aboveground racists. Seemingly benign-sounding terms like "real American," "European values," and "Christian unity" bear new meaning alongside encoded phrases like "racial danger," "nonwhite oppressor," and "rahowa." Understanding the contemporary language of racial propagandists is important to deciphering the true intention behind their words.

These four prime areas of investigation – presentation, message, strategy, and language – can reveal a great deal about the ways that hate speech has been adapted to masquerade itself as useful information and popular culture in cyberspace. We begin by presenting findings about the nature of informational content, specifically, while always keeping in mind the primary target audience of our hosts. As the founder of one of these sites reminds us: "We find that college students in general are more receptive to new ideas, they're more open-minded, and they are willing to get involved in our church...it is often young bright college students who are most receptive to what we say."[117] Along this sentiment, this section focuses on these websites' informational features, news forums, research content, and scholarly signifiers intended for the college crowd. We begin, however, by introducing the primary method used throughout this multi-part investigation.

Frame Analysis

Frame analysis is a qualitative measuring device for exposing how a particular media outlet shapes, packages, and ultimately delivers informational content to the public. The concept of framing is often attributed to Goffman (1974), a sociologist who was interested in the ways that people "locate, perceive, identify, and label" life experiences and current events. Understanding

---

[117] Carol M. Swain and Russ Nieli. Contemporary Voices of White Nationalism in America. (Cambridge, UK: Cambridge University Press, 2003) 238.

that people often compartmentalize the world around them into logical frames led later researchers to wonder whether outside elements, like the media, were actually feeding into or even creating interpretations of their own. For our purposes, frame analysis provides an ideal measuring device for exposing how the various white power websites are shaped by their inscribers to produce the desired interpretation by a mass audience, in this case, young online visitors.

In his extensive work on framing, Entman (2003) posits that, "most frames are defined by what they omit as well as include, and the omissions of potential problem definitions, explanations, evaluations, and recommendations may be as critical as the inclusions in guiding the audience."[118] In other words, a media frame is designed with a purpose to convey a specific understanding of a given issue or idea. White nationalist organizations thrive on this concept in their presentation of "the facts" that support their mission statements and issues but overlook any form of criticism or counter argument. The websites examined in this study clearly applied frames to present carefully constructed messages of anti-Semitism, racism, and white supremacy.

In "White Supremacists, Oppositional Culture and the World Wide Web," Adams and Roscigno attribute much of the success of the white power movement online campaign to their skillful dissemination of the single recurring theme: the "righteous crusades" of white men against the "evil conspiracies" of the nonwhite races. They assert, "It is this juxtaposition of conspiracies with crusades that has provided the dominant recruitment frame and identity for many white supremacist organizations."[119] Certainly, frames of "conspiracies" and "crusades" were highly prevalent within these 26 websites which used them to develop a fearful loathing of the nonwhite races. But there were two over-

---

[118] Robert M. Entman. "Framing: Towards clarification of a fractured paradigm." Journal of Communication, 43 (1993) 51-58.
[119] Josh Adams and Vincent J. Roscigno. "White Supremacists, Oppositional Culture and the World Wide Web." Social Forces, 84:2, (2005) 759-777.

arching messages of white power discourse that emerged within this analysis that superseded these and all other dominant frames. They are the *information* and *uprising* frames.

This chapter is primarily concerned with the information frame, which is defined here as messages that produce racist facts and conclusions with the desired audience, simultaneously furthering the idea that these websites are a trusted source of information. While the propagation of white power-based facts into the mainstream circuit is an essential goal of these websites, the primary function of the information frame is actually to legitimize their overall cause. The earlier theory of information laundering describes an online system that aids in that objective by delivering new prospects to these websites via credible to semi-credible channels of cyberspace (i.e., Google, Wikipedia, You-Tube, blogs) which in turn funnel into other white power domains. However, information frames more specifically shape the internal messages and white power persona in a manner that crafts a respectable and trusted identity in the eyes of online visitors.

The uprising frame, which at times overlaps informational themes, will be the central focus of the next chapter. However, for now it is important to understand how this frame activates another overarching strategy of the white power movement. Messages in the uprising frame collectively assert that the white race is, in fact, the new oppressed minority of the world that must overcome the oppressive nonwhite majority. This expression takes on many forms in the white power domain, but specifically it evokes an underlying sentiment of social rebellion that tends to appeal to the defiant natures of many young adults. In fact, that is precisely the intent of website inscribers. As our analysis of the website forums will later show, the message of a youthful uprising is not only promoted in white power websites, it is also received.

To support these and other overarching findings, this research employed a method of analysis that was designed to identify contextual commonalities among media frames, mission statements, purported research material, and crafted news stories. This study was also interested in gathering quantifiable content that demonstrated the broader trends present in the features and offerings of these 26 sites. These trends collectively signified what was once characterized as a one-dimensional and local movement, reinvented online with all the modern bells and whistles of a vibrant multidimensional global community.

Period of Analysis

In chapter 4 we introduced 26 white power websites that were selected as leading representations of three desired research criteria. Those criteria included the website's frequency of visitation, its affiliation in the arena of white power organizations and causes, and lastly, its representation of modern Internet trends. The contextual and frame analyses of these websites spanned over a period of 12 weeks of investigation, from June 20th 2009, through September 20th of that same year. This particular three-month period, the summer of 2009, was marked by a resurgence of racist and anti-Semitic activity both on the fringe and mainstream circuits. The most poignant example of this spike in hate occurred just over a week before the onset of this investigation when 88-year-old James von Brunn shot and killed an African-American guard in his blocked attempt to take more lives at the U.S. Holocaust Memorial Museum. Von Brunn, a recent recruit of the "Obama birther movement"[120] and longtime voice of anti-Semitic circles, became an instant hero and martyr among the white nationalist base behind these causes, as strongly evidenced in the writings and response of the white power websites. His extremist actions, however, would mark only the beginning of a long summer of renewed racist sentiments in the United States that was largely centered on the race, religion and nationality of the first African-American president, Barack Obama, as well as

---

[120] Sam Stein. "James Von Brunn Apparently Part of the "Birther" Movement." Retrieved June 25, 2009, from http://www.huffingtonpost.com/2009/06/10/james-von-brunn-apparentl_n_214006.html

his Jewish White House staff members and supporters. In actual fact, the preexisting political fever was merely the ideal host for a viral strain of racist ideology that had long been waiting to resurface in American discourse.

In mainstream cases, early examples included legitimate healthcare rallies that began to sporadically reveal an undercurrent of racism beneath banners that likened the black president to an African witch doctor, a Muslim terrorist, a genocidal Nazi leader, a gorilla, the anti-Christ, and even a threat to "White Christian America."[121] Such sentiments in national politics had not been seen quite as often and openly since the 1960s backlash to the Civil Rights era. In the media world as well, prominent voices like radio host Rush Limbaugh were broadcasting statements like, "You put your kids on a school bus, you expect safety, but in Obama's America the white kids now get beat up with the black kids cheering" in his response to a high school incident in Missouri that police authorities determined was non-race related.[122] On the left as well, outspoken religious figure Reverend Jeremiah Wright publicly declared to the press, "Them Jews ain't going to let [the President] talk to me," referring here to President Obama's strong ties with the American Israel Public Affair Committee (AIPAC).[123] However, over this same summer period, while racial and anti-Semitic expressions were bubbling up to the surface of American politics and media culture, a deeper cauldron of hate was beginning to spill over in cyberspace.

---

[121] David Weigel. Scenes from the DC Tea Party. Retrieved September 16, 2009 from http://washingtonindependent.com /38877/scenes-from-the-dc-tea-party-more-photos
[122] Nicholas Graham. "Rush Limbaugh – Obama's America." Retrieved September 16, 2009 from http://www.huffingtonpost.com /2009/09/16/rush-limbaugh-obamas-amer_n_288371.html
[123] Dan Gilgoff. "Rev. Jeremiah Wright Says Jews are Preventing Obama from Talking to him." Retrieved September 4, 2009 from http://www.usnews.com/blogs/god-and-country/2009/06/11/rev-jeremiah-wright-says-jews-are-preventing-obama-from-talking-to-him.html

According to web information company, Alexa.com, which monitors 'three-month averages' in website activity, those same 26 white power sites increased in online visitation between mid-June and mid-September by an average of 31%.[124] Websites like Stormfront went from being ranked the 13,910th most frequented website in cyberspace to the 11,659th, while smaller sites like the New Saxon social network jumped from a #551,440 ranking to #305,608 – a 90% increase in online visitors. In cyberspace, that kind of spike in activity is synonymous with a wildly successful TV pilot or an exploding music scene when compared to the movement at large. But even more so, this increase translates into a direct implication of a movement that had potentially received one-third more prospects and potential recruits in the summer of 2009. Was there a direct linkage between those new radicals of mainstream politics and these underground spikes in extremist racism? Absolutely. And the white power-based rhetoric of these 26 examined websites would provide a strong contextual evidence to prove it.

Method of Analysis

While much of these sites' forums and public-sharing materials were in constant flux over the three-month period, their homepage contents and central features remained relatively unchanged during that time, which allowed for a balanced and steady analysis of these variables. In order to aptly measure the varying degrees by which the 26 websites reflected the information culture of cyberspace, each homepage was carefully analyzed and categorized according to its provisions of five distinct categories: research tools, news sources, links, mainstreaming elements, and scholarly signifiers. For the coding process, a clear definition was needed to identity each of these online features.

---

[124] Information tabulated from the three-month average data of White Power Websites on Alexa.com. Retrieved on September 20, 2009 from http://www.alexa.com/

A research tool consisted of any feature that offered either encyclopedic or scholarly information about matters pertaining to race, religion, nationality, or sexuality. Examples of these included databases of racial terminologies, downloadable articles, and posted statistics – essentially black propaganda material. A news source was deemed as any article, report, or commentary on a contemporary issue. These often were drawn from actual news items or external links to mainstream news which contained some elements of facts, and therefore, fell under the most common application of white propaganda. Next, the provision of links on the homepage was plainly defined as any subheading or picture that leads visitors to another website altogether (most commonly another white power website). Network links by themselves may not denote an informational feature, but collectively they are essential to presenting the white power movement as a larger field of scholarship, interconnected and factually reinforced. The fourth variable called mainstreaming was also vital to this equation. Elements of mainstreaming on the homepage were defined as any feature that either referred or connected to a conventional website or online source. Examples of mainstreaming included direct links to YouTube, or the inclusion of a mainstream news story within the homepage (i.e., an exploited Fox News or CNN article). Finally, scholarly signifiers referred to any identifiable construct or context that, through its association, aimed to academically legitimize that website. Examples of these included noted university affiliations, Ph.D. credentials, library links, and falsely-associated sources like Charles Darwin.

Along these definitions, two separate coders reviewed each of the 26 websites noting their identified inclusions or exclusions of these features. Once both researchers had separately reviewed the entire sample, Scott's Pi was employed as the ideal statistical measuring device for determining the reliability between each coder's findings. This study initially aimed for a minimum 70% level of agreement which Shoemaker (2003) classifies as "good" for the application of Scott Pi.[125] In fact, the intercoder reliability test yielded a Scott's Pi of 84%, which is considered to be an "excellent" level of agreement.

In addition to informational features, this research also aimed to identify a recurring set of "facts" emanating from within such contents, those we call information frames. Of the 26 websites, 21 of them presented informational frames, mostly through news and research content that ranged from topics on illegal Hispanic immigration to Jewish media manipulation, the threat of gay lifestyles in America to local crimes by African Americans. Among these and dozens of other cataloged storylines, this research ultimately identified seven overarching themes repeating throughout these sites over the three-month period. Frames were initially catalogued by news research sub-headings that appeared at least three or more times to confirm a thematic repetition. From that collection, the seven news and information frames identified here represent the most common assertions of the white power movement. The final qualitative analysis section exposes these so-called facts and conclusions, and the underlying messages behind them.

Findings Part I: The Information Trend Line

The 26 websites represent not only a cross-section of the leading voices of white power radicalism around the world, but also a collective shift in their message strategy. Within the information superhighway of cyberspace exists a culture of knowledge seekers and providers with widely-recognized customs, trends, and features. In what might be considered the most sophisticated form of propaganda ever practiced by the white power movement, these 26 sites have modified their own identities (some more than others) to blend in with that new media and informa-

---

[125] Pamela Shoemaker. "Intercoder Reliability." Retrieved on June 10, 2009, from http://web.syr.edu/~snowshoe/content_analysis/ Intercoder_reliability.doc (November 20, 2003).

tion culture. Like a chameleon, the white power website has studied its surroundings carefully in order to change its appearance to match the new online environment. In Table 5.1, we see the initial results of that camouflaging process. Though these are only the external findings from the website homepages, in many ways they are potentially the most significant. That is because for Internet-users, the process of judging a website often occurs upon the initial encounter. If the website meets the current Internet standard of proficiency and flash, users will entrust their intellectual faith to its deeper pages and contents. One of the most recognized indicators of a legitimate website is the inclusion of an up-to-date news source.

Table 5.1 – Collective Sample of 26 Websites: Informational Features	Inclusion Percentage
NEWS SOURCE	81%
RESEARCH TOOLS	69%
SCHOLARLY SIGNIFIERS	58%
NETWORK LINKS	85%
MAINSTREAMING	80%

Out of the collective sample, 81% of the websites offered some form of contemporary news within the homepage. As stated, news items presented in this context are not provided for the mere pleasure of the community. Rather, they serve as the catalysts for sparking racist sentiments out of current events. Over the summer 2009 period of analysis, some of the recurring news events that Americans read about in the mainstream newspapers were simultaneously being covered by these 26 websites. News stories like the national health care debate, coverage of the nationwide "tea party" rallies, the confirmation of Sonia Sotomayor to the Supreme Court, and Congressman Joe Wilson's "you lie" outburst at the president's congressional address were all hot topics *from which* the white power movement was able to draw racial undertones and offer editorial commentary. Other sites focused on more local new stories with noted interest in news that emanated from college campuses, such as the firing of a white professor or affirmative action policy under new review. Other websites, which tended to focus more directly on anti-Semitism, utilized international news like the Israeli-Palestinian conflict to once again the cast the Jews as the cause of a world problem.

Keeping the online visitor in mind, the news items positioned a steady selection of current events intended to manipulate what issues an audience thinks about. This theoretical concept is known as *agenda-setting* (McCombs & Shaw, 1972)[126] and is actually true of most news outlets. With agenda-setting, news outlets like Fox and the *New York Times* each enjoy that journalistic privilege of deciding what is and is not important news to report, and thereby set the national agenda for topical debate. However, the Internet has also been cited by some as providing a balance to leading news selectors and providers (Klein, Byerly, McEachern, 2009), thereby offering a much wider alternative source of information.[127] The white power websites have clearly begun to tap into that journalistic potential, and within their own cyber

---

[126] Maxwell E. McCombs and Donald L. Shaw. "The Agenda-Setting Function of Mass Media." Public Opinion Quarterly, 36 (1972) 176-187
[127] Adam Klein, Carolyn Byerly, and Tony McEachern. "Counterframing Public Dissent: U.S. Coverage of the Iraq Antiwar Movement." Critical Studies in Media Communication, 26:4 (2009) 331-350.

worlds are now setting the new agenda for what online-visitors will be thinking about throughout their day.

While news items tend to speak to the general concerns of a population, *research tools* are usually of interest to particular segments of that society, most commonly college students. Various types of research were featured on 69% of the website homepages, mainly scientific articles, books, and online databases. Websites like the Institute for Historical Review and the Charles Darwin Institute provided faux-academic materials such as research papers on topics that, at first glance, seemed to relate to history, science, and sociology. However, a closer analysis of these articles revealed the true nature of their investigation and special interest. For example, the Family Research Institute (FRI) website offers "Special Reports" and "Scientific Articles" on all matters of homosexuality. The FRI homepage itself is decorated with images of microscopes, a graphic of the human brain, as well as a silhouette of the nuclear family – man, woman, and children. The articles themselves, however, tended to reveal much more about the Family Research Institute than they do about the topics they claim to examine.

The FRI scientists included "in-depth" studies on inquiries like "Homosexual Brains?," "Does Incest Cause Homosexuality?," "Do Homosexual Teachers Pose a Risk to Pupils?," and "Homosexual Sex as Harmful as Drug Abuse, Prostitution, or Smoking."[128] Clearly, it is difficult to imagine any respectable scientist quantifying these types of faux studies with measurable results. However, on a website, the perceived legitimacy of the messenger and the medium is just as important as the message itself. For the typical college freshman, perhaps new to research but familiar with the Internet, an organization like the Family Research Institute sounds like a credible resource and its website appears much the same way. But beneath the surface, the FRI site is built upon homophobic biases and political motivations,

---

[128] Family Research Institute. "Scientific Articles." Retrieved on September 10, 2009 from
http://www.familyresearchinst.org/category/articles/

neither of which have a place in true science. The same axiological principles of investigation apply to the Holocaust denial "historians" whose attempts to debunk the genocide of six million Jews are really motivated by anti-Semitism, or anti-immigration political scientists whose perspectives are guided by white supremacy. Such research is not objective or even subjective in its foundation and approach. Rather, as pure biases, the researchers have already embraced a conclusion about a given topic, and therefore, are incapable of arriving at any legitimate degree of discovered knowledge.

Other examples of research tools included vast databases of encyclopedic information about race, religion, gender, nationality, and sexuality. These were often more outspoken in tone with regard to their racist beliefs and values, but nevertheless, still provided a large collection of user-friendly content. For the target audience, this user-friendliness is an important element because it offers up the "fast food" form of informational data that other Internet databases often provide, and on which the hastier college students have come to rely. Further, the database website design resembles that of other mainstream sites like Wikipedia, a trusted information source for many young adults, and therefore, is subversively applied by domains like Jewwatch and the Vanguard News Network as a disarmingly familiar substitution.

Another important symbol of trusted information is the inclusion of *scholarly signifiers* on the homepage. These tell-tale signs of academic prowess and standing were applied to 58% of the total website sample and were often highlighted by scholarly credentials like masters and doctoral degrees, loose university affiliations, and even looser intellectual associations. For example, websites like the Creativity Alliance and Charles Darwin Research Institute both falsely applied Charles Darwin's name and picture to their cause of racial superiority. Other more contemporary examples of these signifiers included references to sponsoring "academics" like Frank Weltner of the Jew Watch Project, to enhance the standing and perceived credentials of their homepages. While, most readers probably never heard of Mr. Weltner, the Jewwatch website introduces him under the homepage caption, "Historical Statement of our Goals, Focus, and Philosophy by Frank Weltner, M.A. English, Librarian of the Jew Watch Project."[129] Here Weltner's actual identity is not as important as those respectable qualifications he brings to the page. Scholarly signifiers like Weltner's M.A. in English and his librarian standing might inspire trust among academic-minded student visitors.

The Institute for Historical Review site offers its own library and archive section with noted contributors of "articles, reviews, books and essays."[130] Among them, "Tony Martin, professor of African studies at Wellesley College," and "Tom Sunic, author, scholar, and former political scientist and diplomat." Martin and Sunic's scholarly references serve much the same purpose as 1960 white nationalist pioneer, Willis Carto, who published under the penned pseudonym, E.L. Anderson, Ph.D. They are the calling cards of false academic achievement that together signify a more legitimate white power movement. The library signifier is one of the most important elements in this equation because it is the universal symbol of trustworthy information, and librarians are entrusted as the gatekeepers and guides of that content. White power websites utilize these references in order to falsely acquire that same certified and trusted status in the eyes of college students.

While scholarly signifiers are employed to highlight a particular website's academic credibility, *network links* on the other hand are constructed to bolster the impression of a larger field of study of which that site and its content belong. The inclusion of links accounted for 85% of the website sample, the most frequently featured homepage informational item. In the general context of cyberspace, these links connect one white power site to another or to several other hate websites, thereby broadening and uniting the supremacist community across the globe. In the

---

[129] Jewwatch. Retrieved September 3, 2009 from
http://jewwatch.com/ homepage
[130] Institute for Historical Review. "Library & Archives." Retrieved
September 4, 2009 from http://www.ihr.org/main/library.shtml

informational context, however, that same interconnection process helps to extend the notion that the knowledge and viewpoints
found within these homepages are strongly supported by the
identical perspective of another. This infrastructural component
of the World Wide Web has given the white power movement a
newfound mobility and shared stature that it had never had prior
to the information age.

Some of the common links shared by the 26 websites in this
sample is a listing of the "Top 100 Nationalist Websites" which
immediately brings the Internet-user to a colorful page of 100
white power sites, many of which are among the more extreme
on a theoretical spectrum of hate. In fact, the ranking system itself is merely the user-friendly draw to lure online visitors who
can then connect directly to the sites. Many of the network links
of the websites examined in this study interconnect to each other,
such as the KKK homepage that leads directly to the Stormfront
page or the Vinlanders Social Club that links to the White Boy
Society. In any other medium of mass communication, these
competing white nationalist groups rarely share the same geo-
graphic space let alone prospective memberships. However, in
cyberspace the community is much more interconnected, over-
lapping, and therefore, aligned in a common message.

As networks' links steadily blend together the community of
white supremacists, nationalists, skinheads, and neo-Nazis, their
leading websites are simultaneously reaching outward toward the
mainstream media world. The final informational feature known
as *mainstreaming* was utilized by 80% of the entire sample. This
widespread finding is significant because it supports a key element of the information laundering theory by illustrating how
hate websites borrow the content of mainstream news and popular culture websites like CNN, YouTube and Wikipedia. Examples of the mainstreaming phenomenon were found on the National Socialist Movement website homepage that featured di-
rect-linking news stories from the *New York Times,* Fox News, and

the *London Times*.[131] In every case, these mainstream news stories centered around unrelated, but useful white power issues and events such as corrupt Mexican police officers trafficking drugs into the United States, or local assaults carried out at the hands of an African-American assailant. These non-biased news stories take on new meanings when strung together to present a clear narrative of nonwhite crime and corruption. Other mainstream links indirectly addressed conspiratorial narratives, such as an exposé on the White House Chief of Staff, Rahm Emanuel, which highlighted his dual American/Israeli citizenship and father's longtime membership in the Zionist group, the Irgun. At face value, this news story is merely biographical in nature, but its function on a white power homepage is to present the American president's chief of staff as having strong ties to Israel and Judaism. When placed into the context of an anti-Semitic website like the National Socialist Movement, the benign news link feeds into the pre-established theme of Jewish control and Zionist conspiracy in politics. Through a system of mainstreaming, these ideas are not only reflected by elements outside the immediate racist organization, but they appear to actually be supported by the *New York Times* and Fox News, when of course, nothing could be further from the truth.

The ability for a hate site to launder informational content from mainstream sources may, at some point, become a new legal ground upon which hate speech in cyberspace will inevitably be addressed. It raises a new question that concerns both intellectual property and libel law in the realm of network links. Are hate websites both *stealing* and *misrepresenting* the material of another website simply by providing a direct link to its content? In the untamed domain of cyberspace, this question remains to be answered. In the mean time, websites like the Supreme White Alliance continue to build inroads to the mainstream media and popular culture of cyberspace, thus further legitimizing the stature of their own community.

---

[131] National Socialist Movement. NSM News. Retrieved September 10, 2009 from http://www.nsm88.org/

Collectively, the informational features provided by the majority of this sample indicate a white power movement that has changed its uniform appearance from armbands and army boots to briefcases and neckties. In legitimatizing their general exterior, these 26 sites have attempted to validate the content of their interior pages as well. When we examine the primary information and news frames cited from the news and research sections, it is an easy matter to identify the underlying white power belief system that they are steadily attempting to build.

Findings Part II: White Power Facts and Information Frames

As a collective voice, the white power websites presented seven predominant facts about race in America relating to social, political, and cultural issues. While reoccurring themes of racial superiority and resentments tended to overlap within these sites, the so-called truth posited here accounts for those superseding perspectives that helped to frame an overall image of white and nonwhite America in the eyes of website visitors. Many of these information frames were the product of white propaganda (i.e. slanted and misrepresented news reports from mainstream sources), while others were simply the result of well-manufactured research and falsified science. It is important to note that while the following facts may read like obvious fiction in this labeled context, each has been steadily woven from a broad world wide web of misinformation.

"The truth about..." Seven "Facts" Put Forth by the White Power Movement

1. Black people are a deadly threat to White Americans.

A number of news stories centered on the sweeping generalization that all black men present an immediate and deadly threat to white Americans. The "deadly" assertion was arrived at through news articles that depicted gang murders, school shootings, and attempted killings of white men, women, and children all at the hands African-American assailants. The "immediacy" factor was achieved by a constant influx of these stories throughout the 26 websites, thus leaving any regular visitor to draw the logical conclusion that most black men are out to murder the white race. The American Renaissance website, one of the most frequented in the sample, posted a series of articles like "Honor student beaten to death," "Troubled interracial marriage ends in murder, suicide," and "Beating death captured on amateur video."

Strategically, each one of these news stories were initially reported by mainstream news outlets, but then repositioned within close range of one another on the website. This common alignment approach gave the perception of a news fact born of legitimate sources while, at the same time, repeating the theme of 'deadly black violence on the rise.' For many white power sites, this information frame seemed to be directed at a parental audience with an emphasis on black youth violence and the *local* threat. For instance, the White Civil Rights site (WCR) posted headline stories about "White Kids Beaten in Public Schools" and a "Black Serial Killer Caught in Milwaukee." Coupled together in this context, these news events would likely invoke fear and race-based anger in the minds of any protective parent, and that is exactly the intention of these sites. Regarding the school beating story, the WCR site called the incident "another example not only of the horror that White children face in integrated public schools, but the sickening hypocrisy and cowardice of the White adults who refuse to protect them." The single underlying audience being promoted in this sentiment is the White American family that must take personal action against African-Americans in order to protect its own.

This theme building approach was common among many of the websites, though a few were much more direct in their fear-mongering declarations. The Supreme White Alliance site, for example, posted several morbid YouTube videos on its homepage of white murder victims and crime scenes beneath a large caption that read, "The REAL genocide of white people." While many of these stories depicted actual murders committed by

black perpetrators, the notion of a systematic mass genocide of
white people was the pure creation of the websites themselves
and their framing of these news stories as nationwide and related
events. Recalling Entman's earlier explanation of framing, the
notion that "most frames are defined by what they omit as well
as include" applies directly to this type of fact building process.
The overwhelming omission within this particular frame is, of
course, the other local crime stories whose violent assailants were
not black. In 2008, the FBI annual murder rate figures in the
United States reported a total of 14,180 deadly acts had been
committed. Of them, 51.5% of the offenders were black and
46.2% were white.[132] While the number of black offenders was
certainly high in this account, so, too, were the proportion of
white perpetrators, yet almost *none* of the news offered by these
26 sites mentioned a single violent act committed by a white assailant, save one notable exception. The deadly shooting of a
black security guard by white gunman James von Brunn was
covered by several of the websites, however, this particular news
item was framed as a victorious and heroic act, rather than a malicious and cowardly crime.

2. Jews are systematically conspiring to control the United States.

The framing of a Jewish conspiracy was one of the most
commonly manufactured news items presented by the white
power movement. The theme of 'Jews conspiring together' on a
mass scale to control American society was well-rooted throughout these sites in news and informational materials about U.S.
politics, media, business, and education. These four pillars of
American society were posited to be breached institutions by
Jewish manipulators who had already taken advantage of their
elite positions in a conspiracy to destroy a white, Christian nation. In fact, we know this precise message has been constructed

---

[132] FBI. "Murder, Violent Crime Drop in 2008." Retrieved September
12, 2009 from http://www.cbsnews.com/stories/2009/09/14/
national/main5309836.shtml

before, first through the Russian fabrication of the *Protocols of the Elders of Zion* text, and later, by the anti-Semitic news campaign of 1930s Nazi Germany. In both examples, the countries from which the conspiracy charge initially emerged were facing economic and social turmoil, and its leaders pointed to a Jewish scapegoat on which to hang the problems of a nation. Today, amid the current economic crisis confronting the United States, the baseless cries of Jewish conspiracy are once again on the rise.

At the forefront of this frame are websites like Jewwatch.com, which lists literally hundreds of purported Jewish conspiracies at work deep within the fabric of American society. The manipulations they cite range from a "List of America's Jewish Communists" to "the Associations they Dominate," (i.e., "money and business," "politics," "mass media," "universities," etc.) to "Jewish Banking & Financial Manipulations" – an increasingly popular accusation in today's economic environment. Other websites supported these themes through selective news bulletins that featured business and banking scandals perpetrated by people with Jewish names (often in bold text), and an apparent "Jewish Hollywood machine" out to brainwash America. New emphasis was also placed on stories relating to President Obama's Jewish advisors in the White House. The principal suggestion behind these latter stories is that Jewish people are using a black president to promote multicultural institutions in a calculated strategy to bring down the white, Christian society. That same exact conspiracy was crafted one hundred years ago in Russia, via the *Protocols of the Elders of Zion* forgery, just before deadly organized riots called pogroms claimed the lives of tens of thousands of Russian Jews.

One central element to the Jewish conspiracy charge, and perhaps the ugliest of all, was the contention that Jews are exploiting and/or exaggerating the "lie" of the Holocaust as a political means to gain sympathy and favor from the rest of the world. Holocaust denial is something of an obsession among the white power base, especially in websites dedicated to debunking the fact that this systematic genocide had ever occurred. However, even more common among all the white power sites is the

proposed "truth behind the Holocaust" that professes it to be the
secret manipulation tool of the Jewish people. Driving the larger
conspiracy charge, this subframe was supported primarily by
false research that seemed to unearth "new historical facts" on a
regular basis. The Final Solution website, for example, presented
a finding that claimed that "places like Auschwitz, Dachau and
Buchenwald were not in the business of extermination. They
were work camps...Jewish workers were compensated for their
labor with scrip printed specifically for their use in stores, can-
teens and even brothels."[133] Such discoveries, of course, were
never supported by actual facts or reliable sources, but conspiracy theorists tend to overlook these minor elements in their
brand of research. By and large, the Holocaust, which did claim
the lives of 6 million Jews, and *mostly* in places like Auschwitz,
Dachau and Buchenwald, is reduced, in this widely-crafted context, to a bargaining chip that is purportedly being played by the
whole of the Jewish people.

*3. Hispanic immigration is destroying White American culture and liveli-
hoods.*

   If Jews conspire to control American society, and African-
Americans seek to kill off the white race, then Hispanic immigrants intend to wipe out the national culture and steal our livelihoods. That is, according to the various web pages of the white
power movement. Just as Hispanic Americans are among the
fastest growing demographic in the nation, and commensurately
display an increased presence in the U.S. media, so too is their
media presence more frequently seen within the white nationalist
sites. While some news frames positioned Hispanic immigrants as
dangerous criminals, the overriding theme tended to characterize
the Latin *culture* as both invading and destroying a White American way of life. The White Boy Society website depicted the
situation as dire with bulletins like, "Our country is being in-

---

[133] Final Solution. Retrieved September 12, 2009 from
http://www.finalsolution88.com/

vaded from our southern border. Millions of illegal immigrants...steal our jobs and sponge off our taxes."[134] The American Renaissance site highlighted national culture fears through
news stories like "Hispanics now telling us how to speak English"
and "Mexicans turning national forests in marijuana farms."

Other "facts" about immigration included claims that Hispanic Americans, mostly presented as illegal immigrants, are systematically replacing the educational system, language, history,
music, and the local community storefronts with their own Latin
culture. But in reality, these statements had much less to do with
immigration than with an underlying concern about skin color.
As the Vanguard News Network clearly elaborates, "Those
brown-skinned invaders will play a big role in ruining what is left
of our country."[135] Based upon that sentiment, it should come as
little surprise that the cultural and immigration concerns of white
power sites were exclusively directed toward darker skinned
Americans and visitors, while they overlooked immigration that
matriculated via the Canadian border, or cultural diversity that
originated from a European descent. The notion of racial superiority is palpable in this context.

A central theme resting beneath the assertion of a Hispanic
infiltration of American jobs and culture is the idea of "white
dispossession." The fear that white people's livelihoods, posses-
sions, and culture are being taken from them is an essential tool
of racial fanatics that keeps their followers on the alert and in
defense of the white identity. While Hispanic immigrants were
often cast as the central cause of this gradual "dispossession process," other nationalities and races shared in the alleged theft of
white livelihoods as long as they were not of a Caucasian identity. The American Renaissance website, for example, offered a
number of stories that played into this general theme, such as
news that "Asians still earn more than any other racial group" or

---

[134] White Boy Society. Retrieved September 12, 2009 from
http://localwhiteboy.com/home.php
[135] Vanguard News Network. Retrieved August 19, 2009 from
http://www.vanguardnewsnetwork.com/

that there will be "More handouts for Indians." The Stormfront website reported that "Whites [are] becoming a minority in the U.S." while the National Alliance warned "America is a changing country...Bring our troops home and put them on the Mexican border."[136]

4. *Homosexuality threatens the health of American society.*

On both the physical and social level, homosexuality was presented as a growing sickness in American society. In countless ways, gays and lesbians were dehumanized by self-ascribed academics like the Family Research Institute (FRI) and the Council of Conservative Citizens (CCC). These and other hate websites systematically concentrated on the homosexual lifestyle as a disease-ridden subculture and a detrimental condition of modern U.S. society. The Vanguard News Network, for example, asserted that "AIDS [is] still a queer disease that often appears in homosexual men," while FRI scientists posited that homosexuals are more unhealthy than heterosexuals on "just about every measure" including conditions of obesity, asthma, heart disease, depression, alcoholism, and tobacco smoking.[137] The only component missing from these scientific reports, of course, was science itself. With no true methodological data to back up their assertions, groups like FRI relied heavily upon scholarly signifiers built into their website homepage to give the general appearance of academic legitimacy.

However, the "homosexual sickness" frame is not just about reporting on the unhealthy lifestyle of gay men and women. Rather it implies that this "condition" is somehow affecting the rest of American society like the common flu and, as such, must be vaccinated. The FRI site asserted that homosexuality is invading the American schools system, as well as the U.S. armed

---

[136] National Alliance. Retrieved September 1, 2009 from http://www.natvan.com/
[137] Family Research Institute. Retrieved September 1, 2009 http://www.familyresearchinst.org/

forces, and weakening them. The overly homophobic website, God Hates Fags, on the other hand, took a much less scientific approach, and instead focused on religious objections to homosexuality. According to their site, homosexuality is a "plague" that needs to be "totally abolished" from American life. Among its declarations, this rabidly anti-gay church proposed that American "soldiers are dying for the homosexual and other sins of America. God is now America's enemy."[138] Putting hyperbole aside, this statement plays directly into the larger theme of widespread homosexuality infecting American society. The danger of these types of sentiments is that they imply homosexuality is a contamination, or even a contagion, in the health, education, and military safety of this country. Such characterizations not only dehumanize homosexual men and women, but they also promote retaliatory steps to be taken against them even though the gay community has presented no actual threat.

One additional target often associated with the anti-gay frame is the American media. The news and entertainment industry are frequently the focus of radical groups, fringe elements, and even politicians seeking to craft an explanation for the continued success of their enemies and opponents. After all, if gay men and women are lesser human beings, biologically, then how else have so many become leading figures in areas like academia, business, and government? The same problems of logic arise with stereotypical claims of African-American, Jewish, and Hispanic inferiority, yet these racial, religious, and national groups also continue to flourish in present day society. To confront this anomaly, bigoted groups like white power organizations pin their frustrations upon intangible opponents like the media, or social practices like political correctness. With specific regard to the framing of anti-gay sentiments, faceless culprits like "the media" or "political correctness" are presented as the social support system for homosexuality. These are actually codewords meant to insinuate the existence of conspiracies and propaganda as prac-

---

[138] God hates fags. "Marine Funeral Picketing Event." Retrieved September 5, 2009 from http://www.godhatesfags.com/

ticed by newspapers adopting a liberal bias on issues like gay marriage and hate crimes. Groups like the FRI offer counter studies like the one that reported "Gay Roles Up on Broadcast TV" which, in turn, suggested that Hollywood shares in the blame for America's "overly-cultural" state. In front of a 2009 production of the *Laramie Project* – a theatrical recounting of the murder of gay student Matthew Shepard – Westboro Baptist Church picketers held up signs that read, "God Hates Fags! God Hates Fag-Enablers!"[139]

5. *A Black American president is not "one of us."*

For the white power movement, the nomination of the first black American president was in many ways the ultimate public relations gift. The presidency of Barack Obama has given white supremacists a much revived platform for fueling the fires of racism in America through the perceived flaws of just one man. Like every Commander in Chief before him, President Obama has his share of critics and a worldwide press audience to document his challenges and mistakes. However, for the white power movement, each one of this president's mistakes help them to write a narrative intended to judge the 44th president not as the national leader, but as a representative black male. The white power websites examined here have seized the moment with regard to the president's challenges on all fronts, but none so prominently as those rightwing conspiracy theorists who suggest he is not a Christian, an American, or a legitimate president of the United States. The underlying theme constructed out of such claims is that Mr. Obama is not "one of us" because he is black.

The "birther movement," as it has been called, reached public notoriety in the mainstream press during the summer of 2009, but in reality, it emerged in summer 2008 in cyberspace when white supremacists like James von Brunn, and websites like

---

[139] "Laramie Project Rallies." Retrieved on September 12, 2009 from http://www.godhatesfags.com/written/fliers/20091003_Laramie-Project-Boston-MA-Philadelphia-PA-and-Reston-VA.pdf

White Civil Rights, began to insist that Barack Obama's "birth certificate was a fake." The birther or nativist movement was further fueled by accusations from the radical right that then-Senator Obama was really an Arab Muslim pretending to be a Christian American. Today, most of these charges have died out in mainstream politics as several forged Kenyan birth certificates have been exposed, but among the racist cyber dens, the conspiracy lives on in falsified news and research items. For example, the White Civil Rights site continues to run headlines such as "Obama's Citizenship Far from Certain" and "Our First Illegal Alien President" while the racist online encyclopedia, Metapedia, informs its young researchers, "Barack Obama is 'not a natural born American citizen' and was born in Kenya."[140] Beneath these and other questions about President Obama's identity lies a much older and darker stereotype of the black male as somehow being less American than his white counterpart. For today's white supremacists, there is no better spokesperson to embody this revived and contrived characterization than the first African-American president of the United States. As a single representative of Black Americans, whether by choice or by designation, President Obama's character and his political decisions provide precious fodder to feed the pre-established racial stereotypes of modern day hate organizations.

6. *A new white uprising is at the center of today's political issues.*

For decades, racist organizers have sought to inject their own brand of politics into real national issues in an attempt to exploit the public dissent fomenting around a mainstream debate. Today, this same strategy is being applied widely by these 26 hate websites through a virtual mixed bag of political and public affairs in which the white power movement is able to promote its own cause. We have already seen this done with regard to issues

---

[140] Metapedia. "Barack Obama birth controversy." Retrieved August 12, 2009 from
http://en.metapedia.org/wiki/Barack_Obama_birth_controversy

like Hispanic immigration, and affirmative action as it relates to African-Americans. These issues give the white power movement topical causes upon which to vilify an entire race of people, but *without* fear of crossing actual lines of illegal hate speech because they are safe within the realm of politics. More and more, politics in America is becoming a breeding ground for racial extremists who have discovered its opportunistic relation to racial issues. But today that field has expanded to include matters that seemingly have nothing to do with race, racism or social intolerance. Chief among these issues is the national health care debate.

The American Renaissance website frequently focused on the national health care debate as a new white power wedge issue with articles like, "Hispanics, Health Insurance, and Health Care Access." Several websites also championed Rep. Joe Wilson's much publicized "You Lie" moment at the 2009 presidential health care address, interpreting it as a racial slur to President Obama. Sites like Vinlanders Social Club featured the Wilson footage beneath a caption that read, "Joe Wilson is a god damn national hero. Go to his site, write him an e-mail, donate 5 bucks to his campaign. This is a real political bad ass right here. Show some respect." However, other sites focused on newly emerging news items like the H1N1 "swine" flu scare, presented solely as a "Mexican epidemic" that is infiltrating White America, or the sub-prime housing crisis, touted strictly as a result of "black people living beyond their means." Even the growing tea party and town hall protests were positioned as the new epicenter for a white power uprising. Within these national stories, the 26 websites were able to craft racist initiatives through borrowed causes and encoded language. For example, the White Civil Rights site, whose homepage looks and reads like CNN, commented on ugly sentiments that were brewing at a recent Washington, DC "tea-party" protest. They wrote:

> Remember that these protesters are overwhelmingly working White people…This isn't the "Million Man March" of welfare loafers, who have no jobs to worry about and can loaf around with the "brothers" all day long. A crowd this large however is merely the tip of the iceberg. Conservative White people rarely

turn out for political mass rallies. A right wing rally this large in DC is a huge sign that mainstream America is outraged by the trillions in deficit spending and the socialized health care scheme Obama plans to shove down our throats.[141]

This excerpt reveals the white power strategy of adopting issues bigger than their own. Further, the writer uses code words like "Million Man March," "welfare loafers," and "brothers" to denote the image of black people without clearly identifying them in context. The intent of exploiting this and other unrelated political issues is to allow white power websites like the KKK.com to present themselves and their movements as part of a national rebellion against nonwhite races on *all* fronts: economic, social, even national health issues. The true test of success in this "piggy-backing" approach is whether such racist sentiments, which begin here in the outer-fringes of cyberspace, ultimately surface in mainstream outlets in months to come. With regard to political issues like health care and the tea party rallies, earlier evidence indicates that racist ideologies already have bubbled to the surface. From this research, we can look at newly paved avenues for hate like the H1N1 flu or the housing crisis as barometers for measuring white power success in *reframing* these as anti-Hispanic or anti-African American causes, respectively.

7. New evidence proves the White race is biologically superior.

At the heart of all the aforementioned facts is the single belief that has motivated white power extremists for centuries, the white superiority complex. This fundamental belief has been given new life in cyberspace where organizations like the Charles Darwin Research Institute and the Creativity Alliance have sought new information strategies to prove their assertion of white superiority. Chief among them is the biological frame, which contends that new science has provided the final word on racial evolution, superiority, and likewise, inferiority.

---

[141] White Civil Rights. Retrieved on September 9, 2009 from http://www.whitecivilrights.com/

To promote this claim, the Charles Darwin Research Institute relies on bending the scholarly works of a few respected scientists, namely its self-ascribed "founder," thereby suggesting the perceived existence of a body of literature that supports white superiority. Some of the information they provide includes proclamations like "the average mental ability of Africans [is] low, whether they [are] observed or in Africa or in the Americas."[142] Just as the Family Research Institute often attributes the societal acceptance of homosexuality to media bias and influence, the Charles Darwin Research Institute also employs a convenient scapegoat to account for the white power movement's nonbelievers. They write, "Let us be explicit about the problem faced by Darwinian psychology – political correctness." The Institute asserts that Americans typically "censor" themselves from accepting the truth that the white race is biologically superior simply for the sake of being politically correct.

The Creativity Alliance website goes one step further by infusing religion into the racial hierarchy equation. Their site proclaims, "We believe that race is our religion...We believe that the White Race is nature's finest." The concoction of science and religion in this context is a dangerous one for it implies that holy license is granted to followers that choose to act upon their "god-given" rights of superiority. The mission statement of this site is even more troubling because it spells out precisely what form that action should take. They write: "Christianity teaches love your enemies and hate your own kind, while we teach exactly the opposite, namely hate and destroy your enemies and love your own kind."[143] While these words, like the many "truths" offered by these white power sites, are just thoughts on a web page, they teach lessons which occasionally provoke literal interpretations. The Creativity Alliance is no stranger to this grave possibility, for it was one of their own young members that, in 2002, turned

---

142 Charles Darwin Research Institute. Retrieved September 10, 2009 from http://www.charlesdarwinresearch.org/
143 The Creativity Alliance. "Mission Statement." Retrieved on September 10, 2009 from http://www.creativityalliance.com/index.html

words into action by killing two persons of color and wounding nine others, yet these and other hate sites continue to claim no responsibility for such events. On the National Socialist Movement website, one of its news bulletins currently reads, "Actions, Not Words!"

Conclusion

When analysts attempt to understand the minds of radical and racial terrorists like Timothy McVeigh or James von Brunn, the overlying question they often seek to answer is "why." Why do such hateful extremists go a step beyond their internal resentments to actually commit external acts of bloodshed and murder? The answer almost always comes back to some adopted belief system to which they were deeply committed. Perhaps the most alarming finding from the analysis of these 26 websites is the *actual* fact that behind all the informational assertions, news bulletins, research and conspiracy theories, these inscribers of hate are establishing a powerful belief system of their own.

Today's white power mission statement is built upon a foundation of "news and information" rather than the publicity of a street rally hate parade. In cyberspace, social commentary, intellectual debate, and politics are expressed through the language of blogs and news sites, and so this has become the strategic voice box of white power websites as well. But just beneath that foreground, the messages that one draws from the lessons of white power sites like Stormfront or Metapedia.com are easy to comprehend. "America is a changing country," the National Alliance warned us. And this is, no doubt, meant to be a call for national alarm. In their mission statement, the National Socialist Movement (NSM) elaborates on this central theme of the greater community:

> The government cares more about the nonwhites and they bend over backwards trying to please them. You can have all the special rights, and benefits, privileges and free rides as long as you are a nonwhite. The jew media encourages race mixing in all races but their own. Why is that? The reason is their ha-

tred for the Aryan Race. Many people know there is "something wrong" in our nation and in our world, but they just can't nail down the exact causes. It's not just human nature or a sign of the times. There is much more to it than that. If you are old enough you remember a much different America. It was a cleaner, freer, prouder, safer and Whiter America.[144]

In these words lay the modernized foundation for a white power uprising. They suggest that the great White American race is actually *being* changed, unnaturally and unfairly, by "something wrong in our nation." That "something" is the nonwhite community and all that entails. For newcomers to the cause, the NSM website, along with its 25 siblings, has created a vast network of knowledge to prove their theory of a nonwhite oppression threatening traditional White America. Next, we will finally see how these facts and features have resonated with the visitors and members of these sites.

---

[144] National Socialist Movement. "Why you should join the NSM?" Retrieved on September 13, 2009 from http://www.nsm88.org/articles/ whyyoushouldjointhensm.htm

6. A Grassroots Campaign for Hate

If the central purpose of the information frame is to legitimize the cause of white nationalism, the uprising frame serves
but one primary objective as well – to mobilize it. Uprising
frames are those messages of white power discourse crafted to
strike a cord of racial rebellion with online audiences. Not unlike
the alarming rhetoric that is often voiced during legitimate times
of national security crises or local community crime scares, uprising frames carry similar tones of alarm, fear, outrage, resistance,
and action. Only, these responses are not directed toward the
menacing nation or local street gang that threatens the greater
good. Rather, they are focused on an entire race of people – the
nonwhite oppressor supposedly in our midst and invading our
culture. As history has shown when such racist campaigns become well-packaged frames of bigotry, they can quickly turn the
call for alarm among the few into a call-to-arms for the many.
Yet, how does one identify these messages within today's white
power discourse which masquerades as a beacon of trusted information? To answer that question, we peel back the final layer
of the white power movement website — that is, the social and
cultural fold of the public sector of these sites where members
and new visitors intermingle.

If we think of the white power website as a public domain,
then the digital architecture of its design serves a function similar
to the layout of a house or office space. One might argue that a
white power website like KKK.com is both a home and a workplace to the communities that inhabit its pages and fill its forums.
But structurally, these extremist websites are built not unlike
most model facilities. From the outside, the visitor sees the fullest
perspective of a homepage, its features, entrances, interconnected corridors, and exits. As they go deeper into that site, the
main pages are publicly presentable, both appealing in form and
professional in tone. However, like most public domains, these
sites also have an additional space for the informal and unfiltered

content. Beneath the digital exterior of homepage and features, it is the social forums that serve as the basements of white power culture – never seen upfront, yet always thriving with activity at the interiors of these sites. And it is within these public-fed spaces where we will find the truest nature and character of this particular online community.

While even white power websites will sometimes post "rules" or "terms of service" within the open forums they house, these artificial measures do little to curb the actual extremist and radical sentiments of members and visitors who use the anonymous platform as a soundboard for voicing hateful diatribes. Here, one can truly feel the pulse of online hate beating toward blatant cries of resentment, disgust, rage and hostility towards all nonwhite races. The thematic message of white uprising encapsulates most of these sentiments, but through the unabridged expression of members who hold nothing back when they tell others:

> "Get yourself a pistol. Preferably like a 44 mag, them niggers heads are hard."[145]

> "The "6 million lie"… Jews are the lawyers and the judges. But we know the problem and we know that we can solve it if we eradicate them."[146]

> "The sooner race war begins, the sooner North America will be partitioned along ethnic lines."[147]

> "There's a revolution brewing…America is in distress, a call-to-arms."[148]

---

[145] Hammerskin Nation.. "General Discussion Area." Retrieved September 17, 2009 from
http://hammerskins.net/forum/index.php/topic,2289.msg 21191.html#msg21191
[146] "Jews Destroyer of Cultures." Retrieved September 17, 2009 from
http://hammerskins.net/forum/index.php/topic,235.0.html
[147] "On the Verge of Civil War in America?" Retrieved September 17, 2009 from
http://www.stormfront.org/forum/showthread.php?t=626602

Clearly, it is within these public spaces where, at last, we expose white power culture at its core.

The Public Domain: Letting Them "Own It"

From a theoretical perspective, the new public-centered core of the white power movement represents a great shift in the strategy of racial propagandists. Whereas prior to the Internet, groups under the white nationalist banner would build their movements by recruiting through *their own* message, the online forum has changed that entire approach. Now, the messages of racial hate are largely developed by website members and visitors amid daily online interactions. In this way, the white power movement has adopted a modernized grassroots approach by providing the space for a natural public discourse about racism to bloom. Of course, the organizers certainly aid in that growing process through their clever designs of forums and discussion boards that center on catalyst topics like "Science, Technology, and Race," "Jokes and Stories," "Revisionism," "Recruiting Tips/Tools," "White Freedom," "Fighting," and "Doomsday." These actual subheadings are merely the seeds for conversation that lead into much deeper and darker discourses among members whose ongoing responses can carry on in vitriol for page upon page. Other examples of this catalytic approach to home-grown racism include the ability for visitors to post their own daily pictures onto online community bulletins, upload amateur videos, join online radio discussions, and sell various items in the classified ads.

The design and implementation of these interactive features are important to the white power movement's new recruitment strategy for two reasons. First, such features reflect the character of the net generation, specifically. As noted earlier, a common characteristic of today's young adults is their insistence on being

---

[148] White Boy Society. "Forums." Retrieved September 17, 2009 from http://www.whiteboysociety.net/e107_plugins/forum/forum_viewtopic.php?1671

active participants in their own media worlds. This was already established in the interactive evolutions seen in online gaming, movies, and music. But like the creators of these media sensations, the white power movement has also calculated that today's youth want to be *a part* of their online community – they want to shape it rather than feel they are being shaped by it. As such, the inclusion of member forums, chat rooms, and video interaction is merely an acknowledgement of the new language spoken by the net generation.

The second reason why an interactive grassroots approach is of such value to white supremacists relates to the mobilizing power of *suggestion* in activating a social response. As many political and public relations specialists are well aware, the subtle suggestion of a social position can often resonate much more so with an audience than the outright promotion of it. Psychologically, the former tends to require a greater degree of participation and thought process to arrive at an opinion, as opposed to being directly told what to think. In truth, the mental journey from the consideration of an issue, to the stance taken on it, is somewhat "doctored" in this paradigm, because the initial thought process did not begin with the audience. Rather it was subliminally introduced to them by the inscriber, in this case, the white power movement, through targeted questions and select subheadings, topics for online discussion, and of course, the site's initial news and information contents that spark later debate among members. These foot-in-the-door techniques are the manufactured catalysts for igniting a falsely-organic style discussion about race. Through these orchestrated debates, suggestions inevitably become "self-realized" facts, sinister questions produce validated answers, resulting in an audience that ends up "owning" the debate. As for the new and fully developed racist sentiment, its point of origin becomes irrelevant. The journey is made complete when those initial visitors-turned-members ultimately become the new leaders of the cause. In fact, in their minds, they initiated it.

Method of Analysis

As in the prior investigation of the information frame, this section's structural analysis begins by locating and quantifying the types of features that crafted a cultural environment among these 26 white power websites. In particular, the research examined social outlets that spoke to a younger online visitor and potential member of the community. Each homepage was carefully categorized according its provisions of five culturally-based categories of interactivity: convergence, merchandising, memberships, public forums, and kid's features.

For the coding process, convergence was defined as any multimedia feature offered by these sites including video-posts, online radio podcasts, white power music downloads, and playable video games. Media convergence appeals directly to the multitasking minds of the net generation and is an essential feature for presenting the white power homepage as an interactive online community. Next, merchandising features were straightforwardly defined as any white power paraphernalia sold through these websites. These can be commodities and racist oddities sold either by the host organization or its members but the primary function of their virtual inclusion is to market the expression of a white supremacist identity. Next, the membership feature was defined as any sign-up capacity found on the homepage, whether it be a mandatory 'member sign-in' space or optional community sponsorships like donations or support clubs. The underlying purpose of such features is to build a more solidified white nationalist front, increase the size of the organization, and to acquire funds for a variety of nefarious purposes. Like official memberships, the public forum feature is also employed for the purposes of community-building, but by less formal means. Public forums are defined as any website feature in which visitors or members are able post their own written comments either in real time chat rooms or daily discussion boards. In many ways, the social forum is the centerpiece of the white power online community serving as both the catalyst and hotbed of racist expression. Finally, the inclusion of kid's features on the white power site was defined as those online offerings solely developed for the attraction of minors who visit the website. These adolescent attractions are fairly easy to recognize, for whom else are features like games, puzzles, cartoons and rock music intended? In addition to these variables, other indicators of a youthful directive include forums offered under subheadings like "kids," "youth corps," "teens" and "students," clearly meant to entice that younger crowd.

The potential inclusion or exclusion of these culturally-designed features was measured in the same dual-coding fashion as those informational variables of the prior chapter. Using the statistical intercoder reliability test of Scott's Pi again, the researchers yielded a strong 82% level of agreement in their separate observation of these features. Beyond features of the homepage, this research section also sought to address an even greater contextual challenge in examining the uprising frame. Like the information frame, the messages of a white power uprising were imbedded in recurring sentiments that were driven by repetitious patterns of discourse. As previously stated, among the online forums and blogs of these 26 websites, a public discourse drives most common sentiments of anger, resistance, and mobilization. These outlets of visitor-based expression are always in constant flux of dissemination from their initial posting to the string of responses that follow, modifications, removals and eventual replacement by other forums from all over the world. In this sporadic and often transitory form of communication, it is nearly impossible to characterize an entire sample of content that is always fluctuating, much like the erratic flow of an actual conversation. Instead, this research sought to examine the broader shape of those unfiltered messages, and the language of their cultural expression.

Message Formation & the Language of White Power Culture

We can learn a great deal about the white power culture by qualitatively investigating the language and rhetorical patterns of its visitors and inscribers within their "marketplace of ideas."

Specifically, this research examined identified uprising frames that were prevalent among many public forums, blogs, and video posts observed early in the investigation. In particular, the language that emerged from these cultural breeding grounds of racist ideology revealed the white power base to be one of established rhetoric, axioms and codewords. Recalling from chapter 1 that existing legislation in several U.S. states presently outlaws the type of hate speech that incites violent action, the resulting language of white power websites is often expressed through careful innuendos and symbolic codes. In other cases, however, some of the language could be viewed as illegal if scrutinized by certain courts of law that prohibit "fighting words." Through selected examples, this research will identify some of these leading linguistic trends and the meanings behind their use in rallying violent action among the young, white masses.

Aside from language, the use of the framing device known as *binary discourse* will also be analyzed in terms of its overwhelming application and presence within these forums. Binary discourse is the process of presenting a message along the lines of two terms or concepts such as weak and strong, guilty and innocent, black and white. According to Coe et al (2004), binary discourse allows an inscriber to craft oppositional positions on a given issue where one side is usually given a "moral power" over the other.[149] Of course, the very act of dividing any issue into two distinct choices is a strategy for propaganda because it essentially simplifies complex issues like race and religion into virtual "sides" and, ultimately, implies to the recipient that they must associate with the right (or white) side. In addition to binary discourse, two newly identified devices of racist expression will be presented among the final set of findings, *message escalation* and *socialized hate speech*. Collectively, these message styles helped to promote the themes of white power uprising like stoking fear, inspiring aggressive ac-

---

[149] Kevin Coe, David Domke, Erica S. Graham, Sue L. John, and Victor W. Pickard. "No Shades of Gray: The Binary Discourse of George W. Bush and an Echoing Press." Journal of Communication, 54:2 (2004) 334-252.

tion, or even suggesting holistic solutions like racial segregation, exile, culture wars, or genocide.

Findings Part I: The Cultural Trend Line

Whether the online visitor enters a white power website seeking information or community, the length of their stay, or likelihood of return, will undoubtedly depend upon how much they identify with the culture of the homepage. This is true of most media outlets that are designed to attract repeat customers. For the 26 white power websites, the inclusion of popular online features like public forums and convergent media encourage new visitors to acclimate themselves within the culture of the supremacist community. In Table 6.1, it becomes evident that the foundation building for that social acclimation process has been well-established by these leading websites of the white power movement.

Table 6.1 – Collective Sample of 26 Websites: Popular Cultural Features	Inclusion Percentage
PUBLIC FORUMS	78%
MEMBERSHIP	81%
CONVERGENCE	85%
MERCHANDISING	69%
KID'S FEATURES	46%

Among the most applied variable within this circle of sites, the *public forum* was featured by 78% of the sample. Public forums, cited earlier as the strategic catalysts of white power hate speech, were commonly directed toward specific pockets of the community. Select forum categories typically identified potential parties under subheadings like "Fellow Patriots," "Parents," "Women," "Fellow Christians," and "Law Enforcement." The

Stormfront website, for example, offered several sections for the educated visitor interested in engaging matters like "Theology," "Poetry," "Science, Technology, and Race." Stormfront also encouraged visitors to engage in forums based on everyday family matters and issues seemingly unrelated to race. Visitors might discuss finances in the "Money Talks" section, or get cardiovascular tips in "Health and Fitness," or share parental advice in the "Homemaking" and "Education and Home schooling" forums. In fact, next to adolescent-related themes, parental topics were among the most popular forum of the sample.

While most forums seemed to normalize the white power cause beneath the banner and banter of kitchen table topics like children's education, other sites played more directly to the base of the movement. In the Hammerskin Nation website, incendiary discussion boards like "race traitors in the family" and "kikes at it again" lit fuses among members eager to share racist rage. What is potentially most troubling about these forums is not only the level of reviling and hate teeming within them, but even more so the fact that like minds who share these thoughts have been brought together. And, as later examples will show, these written forums can foster the same type of hateful spirit and contagious belligerency as an angry mob.

In addition to building social connections, a majority of the sites sought to indoctrinate new recruits by offering a *membership* sign-up feature. In all, 81% of the sample provided some form of user sign-up or membership option, including donation arrangements and social meeting invitations. For most Internet-users the practice of signing up for website access is an afterthought – a brief detour en route to the central site itself. However, most Internet users do not realize that, for the website or sponsoring organization, that sign-up option is a delivery system whereby they receive new member emails, private information like addresses, and even money. For a white power website, the same features also helped to construct an active support system and community outreach among fellow supremacists. In most examples, the websites examined here did not require an initial sign-in page to access the rest of the community. Rather, these sites offered either additional membership options or sign-up requirements to allow access to specific features, like member forums. In order to gain full entry into every corner of these spaces, this research had to provide a form of its own email and password. Following this brief exchange a series of follow-up emails are sent to the address provided, including messages from the community, solicitations for donations, and meeting announcements. Other websites, like the KKK homepage encourages visitors to "get involved" by attending national events or starting their own campaigns locally.[150] In this way, the membership/sign-up function can be viewed as that first step taken beyond the digital community and toward the concrete one. Though most visitors do not realize that they have taken that step simply by signing in, they have, in fact, allowed the white power movement to get their "feet in the door" toward building a relationship with a user that might someday materialize into something more substantial.

Media *convergence* is another cyber trend that is highly prevalent among many online communities today, and as such, has been adopted as a necessity in most social websites. The white power movement is no exception, offering its own technically-savvy features on 85% of its leading websites, including everything from online radio podcasts to video-uploading and direct online gaming. Again, these convergent media are not only the digital indicators of a sophisticated homepage, but also the virtual language through which the net generation is accustomed to communicating via creative, multimedia interactions. Some of the most common uses of convergence in the white power domain include broadcasting audio clips of hate music concerts or video feeds of interviews with white supremacist leaders like David Duke or Don Black. The Creativity Alliance website offers its own regularly programmed videos through "CA-TV" or Creative Alliance Television, which is actually a direct link to their YouTube page.

---

[150] Ku Klux Klan. Retrieved September 10, 2009 from http://www.kkk.com/

Figure 6.1[151] **– CA-TV**

Visit CA-TV at

The employment of YouTube for the purposes of providing video feeds to the white power community was by far the most common application of media convergence within these 26 websites. Through the same function, media convergence itself becomes another form of mainstreaming through which these propagandists are using connections to socially conventional domains, like YouTube, in order to legitimize their own spaces. In terms of the young Internet-user who is already familiar with YouTube, the mere appearance of its (borrowed) affiliation on a website, like the Creativity Alliance, only makes those racist sentiments expressed on CA-TV seem all the more socially acceptable.

Like media convergence, online *merchandising* also allows a social movement or organizational website to communicate its culture both to and among its members. Of the hate sites examined in this study, 69% established the sale of white power paraphernalia, the majority of which was clearly geared toward appealing to younger customers. Items such as neo-Nazi computer mouse pads, White Boy Society tee-shirts, White Aryan Resistance music CDs, backpacks, and other merchandise collectively revealed

---

[151] Creativity Alliance. "Video Downloads." Retrieved September 10, 2009 from http://www.creativityalliance.com/video.htm

a thriving culture of "white pride" being bought and sold in this online marketplace. Websites like Stormfront provided classified ads for members to seek and sell various items to other visitors like an "Authentic Hitler Youth Knife." Other ads were far less benign, such as a posting for "Survival/Tactics/Weapons/ Firearms/Etc." In the surrounding context of a popular white uprising, such merchandise carries an alarming implication and frightening potential.

By and large, however, the majority of the merchandise consists of items like clothing, posters, and music which are typically meant to be worn, pinned up, or played. Such products are not sold merely for the sake of turning a profit, but rather these loud and expressive items are specifically intended to turn heads. The sale or encouragement to sell white pride merchandise that can later be seen or heard by others is another form of foot-in-the-door technique, aimed almost entirely at younger audiences. Here, the goal is to appeal to their cultural style and taste as an initial means of branding the white power look and sound among the net generation. By no means are these websites merely selling a tee-shirt. They are selling the movement.

Finally, 58% of the websites provided cultural applications that were unmistakably intended for use by younger audiences – children to be precise. These *kid's features* fully reveal an alarming youth-recruitment strategy, evoking memories of the Hitler Youth brigades of 1930s Germany. Today, white power websites have reinvested their time and money toward reaching the young minds of this generation. The new youth brigades are found in sites like KKK.com which has built its own "Knights Party Youth Corp."[152] The Women for Aryan Unity homepage features several images of young blond-haired and blue-eyed girls who proudly represent a new kind of female activism in the name of modern Aryanism. And the National Socialist Movement now

---

[152] "Knights Party Youth Corp." Retrieved September 4, 2009 from http://www.kkk.bz/youthcorp.htm

offers a social forum for its "Viking Youth Corp."[153] These mili-
tant-sounding kid's clubs offer a disturbing blend of adolescent
fun mixed together with racist jokes and bully-mongering.
Within many of the white power sites, the new tone being set for
a youthful white America is one of pride – white pride – but also
of refuge. These websites are presenting themselves as a virtual
kid's safe haven from the stress and dangers of nonwhite America. In addition to social forums, other sites offer more interactive
features that speak to the everyday interests of children. Amuse-
ments like cartoons and puzzles, or comic books that depict white
warrior superheroes are intended for those young and impressionable minds who are already accustomed to such mediums of
entertainment. For teenagers, more mature online games such as
"Shoot the fags" and "Kaboom – Arab Training Game" share
themes of aggression and violent actions not so unlike that which
is found in typical video games, but designed along a "racial
war" narrative.

Ultimately, these various cultural features each carry the
same function beneath all of the games, cartoons, forums, video-
feeds, and merchandise they provide. Whether expressed
through the cyber version of friend making, content sharing, or
style adopting, the underlying objective is the end goal of identity
building. But, as the final set of findings will show, the true white
identity that is being communicated through these various cultural formats is not one of national pride, or racial custom, or
religious inspiration. Rather, it is a distinction of character born
from the spirit of social intolerance, racial resentment, and violent inclination.

Findings Part II: White Power Language

Rahowa! This is the secret mantra of the white power movement shared by both Klansmen and neo-Nazis alike. And like the
white power homepage that presents only the outermost layer of

---

[153] "Viking Youth Corps." Retrieved September 4, 2009 from
http://www.nsm88.org/youth/vycjoin.html

the online community, the word rahowa is just an abbreviation for a much darker cause. Rahowa is a battle cry that stands for Racial Holy War. And whether a movement of white supremacy is presented as a religious calling, social network, or a patriotic façade, the inscription of "rahowa" in that site's mission statement underlines its true purpose. As the "Five Fundamental Beliefs of the Creativity Alliance website illustrates, "To the fulfillment of these religious beliefs, We Creators forever pledge our Lives, our Sacred Honor, and our Religious Zeal. RAHOWA!"[154]

Like the violent call for a racial holy war, other radical initiatives have been carefully encoded into a subversive language that is common in this online society. More than just a mode of expression, language itself can also serve as a cultural bond between people, and particularly within a youth culture that is accustomed to using slang in their daily communications. The slang of the white power subculture is no different, and is often used to accentuate one's identity within the group. Codewords represent a secret handshake and a shared understanding among members that they are part of an underground circle. For the disenfranchised student or outsider, this is an ideal community because it is built upon anti-establishment viewpoints which appeal to a social outcast. Familiar themes like rebellion, retaliation, and a protective brotherhood are expressed through various slang-like codes found in nearly every one of the reviewed websites.

Among the most prominent codewords are popular acronyms like ZOG, ROA, and WPWW. Z.O.G. stands for Zionist-Occupied Government and is used to describe the American government as being overrun by Jewish influence, or Israeli government and organizations that purportedly manipulate U.S. politicians, or just the Jewish people at large. Here, we can see how national/political terms like Zionist or Zionism are used to inadvertently denigrate the Jewish people. Examples of this

---

[154] Creativity Alliance. Retrieved August 20, 2009 from
http://www.creativityalliance.com/index.html

codeword used within the Stormfront.org forum include, "It will be easy for the ZOG to take down a bunch of small targets instead of 1 huge 1" and "Death To ZOG!"[155] Here, as in other references, the Jewish people are presented as a regime-like threat, a perilous global enemy with colonialist intentions. Another Hammerskin Nation forum characterized the U.S. economy as part of the "*zog* machine."[156]

The R.O.A. and W.P.W.W. acronyms promote practically the same sentiments: "Race Over All" and "White Pride World Wide," respectively. These phrases are common rally cries within white power domains like Volksfront.com and the New Saxon social networks. The white unity themes they signify are often the closing salutations of member forums, like one blog that ended, "...the Aryan code is strong and shall not be taken from us – WPWW!" Even more common than the use of verbal acronyms is the employment of numeric symbols. References to the numbers 14, 100, 4/20, and 311 are common and prevalent extensions to online screen names (i.e. Kevin14 or Rahowa420). The number 14 refers to the underground motto of the white power movement expressed in "14 words": "We must secure the existence of our people and a future for white children."[157] According to the Anti-Defamation League, the 100 or 100% numeric signifies "an individual's pure Aryan or white roots," while 4/20 is a celebration of Hitler's April 20th birthday. The 311 numeric stands for 3 K's (the 11th letter of the alphabet), thereby representing the KKK. These and other numbers are often flagged like gang colors, and featured as part of white power tag names, merchandise, or even tattoos. Their secret meanings are meant to signify a bond between those racist members that display them.

---

[155] Stormfront. "Forums." Retrieved September 8, 2009 from http://www.stormfront.org/forum/search.php?searchid=7917802
[156] Hammerskin Nation. "Forums." Retrieved August 22, 2009 from http://www.hammerskins.net/
[157] "Hate Symbols." Retrieved August 22, 2009 from http://www.adl.org/hate_symbols/default.asp

However, not all codewords are culturally encrypted as numeric or acronymic symbols. Other words or phrases are employed for the purpose of softening the message of white power
along more politically-acceptable or verbally-inconspicuous
terms. For instance, the Council of Conservative Citizens (CCC)
forum regularly features the descriptor "conservative minded
European-Americans" which really translates to 'white people.'
The CCC domain that aspires for a higher standing within the
political arena cannot communicate through blatantly racist sentiments like "white power" and instead uses loaded language and
codewords. One forum member commented on recent changes
in his local community: "I see what multiculturalism has
done."[158] Here, multiculturalism, decoded, really infers 'race
mixing' which is presented by many CCC members as harming
the American community. Other examples of "benign" language
include terms like "White unity," "Christian society" and
"Americanism." At first glance, these words may suggest racial,
religious, and patriotic communities with which to identify, but
in truth, they really denote an ideological line of supremacy that
comes with the territory.

Findings Part III: Crafting the Uprising Frame

The language of the white power culture, either encoded or
explicit, relays a belief system that strengthens the line between
notions of supremacy and inferiority while igniting the greater
cause of a racial uprising. One of the most prevalent positions of
the white power movement, the uprising frame, has been observed through several examples of this often violent call-to-arms.
However, in addition to the message itself, the style of its mass
communication, what we call message formation, reveals rhetorical patterns that are highly functional in this discourse. For instance, the communicative pattern known as binary discourse
presents opposing language within a single sentiment, but it func-

---

[158] Council of Conservative Citizens. Retrieved August 23, 2009 from
http://cofcc.org/

tions to heighten concepts like superiority and inferiority, oppressor and oppressed, and good and evil. The uprising frame exemplifies a binary discourse, in and of itself, which asserts that the *white race is the oppressed minority* that must overcome *the oppressive nonwhite majority.* In this section, other white power rhetoric is put under a microscope in order to examine the messages it conveys, but even more so the manner in which those positions are presented for public consumption. This is an investigation of the nature of hate speech in the public online forum. Specifically, the mass communication of racial uprising frames were formed through three predominant communicative patterns: message escalation, the socializing of hate speech, and the crafting of divisive binary discourse.

Message Escalation

In a word, Matt Hale describes his racial movement as one of "rebellion." Speaking about his younger recruits, he says, "they're rebelling against the prevalent notions of our time, notions such as that all men are created equal, notions such as that we're simply all Americans, or that we should all just get along."[159] In fact, within most of the examined sites, the mission statements promote some form of this exact message. Examples include the KKK site that referred to its cause as "a grassroots movement to take back America," implying that the country has been taken from the white people. Among its other goals, the Klan aims to stop white people from being "victimized by the entertainment industry," "abolish all discriminative affirmative action programs," "break through the liberal wall that surrounds American colleges," and order the "reclaiming of our schools."[160] These messages use words like "discriminative," "victimized,"

---

[159] Carol M. Swain and Russ Nieli. Contemporary Voices of White Nationalism in America. (Cambridge, UK: Cambridge University Press, 2003) p. 238
[160] Ku Klux Klan. "Our Goal." Retrieved September 8, 2009 from http://www.kkk.bz/ourgoal.htm

"break through," and "reclaiming." Words that suggest the white community has been wrongfully oppressed and must now take action as an uprising white minority.

From these organizational cues, the public discussion that follows within the forums, blogs and convergent media reflect similar, if not stronger tones of rebellion against the nonwhite oppressor. Stormfront members frequently reflect these rebellious sentiments in seemingly non-race-related forums: From *Money Talks:* "the Jew won't need a middle class in my opinion…they will eradicate all whites and rule forever." From *Health and Fitness:* "The majority of the bodybuilders were black, and those few that were White, were tanned so heavily that they too looked black…Why am I not surprised by this? Yet another thing we the White men created being taken away from us." From *Youth:* "My school has about ten blacks in it, and my English class is purely white. Yet the school sees it is applicable to have us learn about the black culture. Not only that, but we never read anything specific about white culture. We never learn about *our* European heritage."

While these racist grievances might promote an uprising by themselves, they are merely the activators of a communication pattern that is unique to the online forum. For every statement made in a public forum, numerous responses follow from other members resounding even louder themes of white-oppression, Jewish conspiracy, black violence, etc., until eventually aggressive action is suggested. Returning to Stormfront, such suggestions included sentiments like "once white America understands what has happened to it, it will already be too late, we'll be Africans/Mexicans." From this, a follow-up response relayed: "RAHOWA seems almost inevitable and the more of us that are still around to fight it the better." While not every forum is inevitably inflamed by another member's promotion of violent action, the online potential to post any series of responses often leads the single forum into a snowball effect, in which the initial sentiment collects increasingly hateful rhetoric from one respondent to the next. The result of this spiraling process is a rhetorical pattern that the research identified as *message escalation.*

Through message escalation, dominant themes like oppression and rebellion complement one another as they are volleyed in a natural succession, from one blogger to the next. On the New Saxon forum, one visitor shared ten reasons why she hates black people with the community. Among them, she writes, "They are welfare hogging pieces of sh*t. When someone actually needs a little help from welfare, they usually cannot receive it due to all the spooks living off of everyone else's work." This sentiment is clearly framed by the prevailing theme of white oppression, in this case with regard to welfare support being exploited by black oppressors. In the later responses, however, the oppression frame escalates into more belligerent themes. One visitor writes, "I also despise those monkeys" followed by another misspelling respondent who pontificates, "There stupid and inferior." Finally, the last posting reads, "Kill them."[161] While such words printed on banners and tee-shirts are likely to command fear and publicity from the local community, in the forum platform, they can escalate organically from anonymous postings in which "everyday racists" are free to join the greater mob in expressing intolerance.

Socializing Hate Speech

The phenomenon of turning the bitter opinions and emotions of racist hate speech into a social and communal platform is a two-part process. It begins with a user that expresses their racist, anti-Semitic, or homophobic ideas within the confines of a non-aggressive conversational environment. These discussions often relate to settings and subject matters seemingly benign in nature like the classroom, workplace, sports field, stock market, movie theatre, or kitchen table. However, the second stage of the socializing process occurs within the language itself where typical sentiments like school frustration or music tastes are conflated with racial tirades or seemingly harmless observations about 'the

---

[161] New Saxon. "Forum." Retrieved September 12, 2009 from http://newsaxon.org/public/forum/topics/id_1/title_General/page_7

Jews' or 'black people.' Snow et al. (1986) called this communicative style *frame bridging*, whereby the inscriber aligns an unrelated issue into the narrative of the central conflict or cause.[162] This alignment enables the source to present the illusion of a unilateral conflict, support, or in this case, opposition to a larger group of enemies.

Socialized hate speech is the common vernacular among the youth dynamic of the white power websites. Within several teenage forums, this message formation was observed with regard to topics like high school cliques, styles, and racial stereotypes. For instance, many student-based discussion boards commented on cultural topics like rap music. Through this platform, however, the discussion quickly branched out into the criticisms of "black music," African-American styles, and other stereotypical observations. Soon, the process of frame bridging fully evolved into a forum-wide denouncement of the black culture. What began as a social conversation quickly transforms into a temper tantrum.

On the Stormfront website, one of the leading hangouts for white power youth, a subheading under the sports forum reads "Football 2009." Its initial posting reads, "Is anyone else a football fan!? I love college the most but also watch some NFL." As the responses amass, one below the other, many of them focus on the 2009 football season. However, it is not long before other posts begin to digress into racial questions such as, "Is it a white man's sport at all now?" or comments like "Negro Felon League." As the unrelated concepts of football and race contextually bridge together, they fortify larger themes in the Stormfront web community. One of the final "Football 2009" commentaries reads,

> I can't believe how many idiots are on this site. So you are going to spend your money to watch a bunch of negroes run and

---

[162] David A. Snow, E. Burke Rochford, Jr., Steven K. Worden, and Robert D. Benford. "Frame Alignment Processes, Micromobilization, and Movement Participation." American Sociological Review, 51:4 (1986) 464-481.

jump and help finance their college tuition and pro multi million dollar contracts...You are white race traitors.[163]

Like Stormfront, the Hammerskin Nation site also provides popular cultural forums that quickly become social breeding grounds for inflammatory hate speech. In "Music and Events," a forum pertaining to the "2008 Hammerfest" heavy metal music concert began, "This years Hammerfest will be held in Texas...Hotels, directions, and band listings will be posted soon." However, after three pages of concert talk regarding the "all white, all proud event," the social excitement gave way to the usual exchanges of hate speech. Under the pretext of the upcoming music festival, respondents began to write, "we won't stay at a crazy ass, nigger filled Motel 8!," "hahahaa, just changed my avatar, got sick of the hanging nig in my tree," "f*ck the jew-nigger system," and "Sieg Heil 88/14!!!"

The Volksfront forums bring together chapter members from all over the world, and as such, find common bonds upon which to communicate universal interests. For instance, the Christian Identity forum seemingly inspires conversations about the Christian faith and its relation to family and social life. However, these forums also follow the established pattern of socialized hate speech by building rhetorical bridges between matters of Holy Scripture and white supremacy. One forum featured several members trading verses of the bible, until someone offered, "Though not scripture, I found this quite interesting: Adam is originator of our white species."[164] From there, the dialogue shifted from holy benevolence to hateful elation.

Without the bigoted overtones that ultimately develop in these topical discussion boards, third party visitors or new members might find few differences between the atmosphere of white power forums and the mainstream chat rooms they regularly

---

[163] Stormfront. "Sports Forum." Retrieved September 11, 2009 from http://www.stormfront.org/forum/forumdisplay.php?f=169
[164] Volksfront. "Forum." Retrieved September 10, 2009 from http://www.volksfrontinternational.com/board/showthread.php?t=913

frequent. These multi-participant communication spaces are often conventional in subject matters like sports and music, and even friendly in tone among the members, thus normalizing the feel of the community. However, the regular spouts of racial rebellion and anti-establishment rants, common among adolescents, are also welcome here. In fact, for the white power movement, they are an encouraged custom. The sharing of hate speech is a regular social pastime for racists who have celebrated its expression at white power festivals, skinhead rock concerts, neo-Nazi bonfires, KKK chapter meetings, and now, online social circles.

Crafting Divisive Binary Discourse

One of the central building blocks to constructing the uprising frame is the contextual polarization of the white and nonwhite communities. In the realm of white power cyberspace, the polarization process is most commonly practiced though a communicative pattern called binary discourse. With binary discourse, any subject matter can potentially deliver a mobilizing message of rebellion to its visitors by positioning the white identity as directly contrasting to nonwhites, and leaving no gray area on which to suggest a common ground. The steady expression of binary terms within the various forums and blogs helps to promote the acceptance of racial differences and disagreements over all other perspectives. Berlet and Vysotsky (2006) called this common view of the white supremacist community "dualism." They write:

> Dualism is the idea that the world is divided into the forces of good and evil with no middle ground...The White Supremacist movement presents the world as a place where heroic warriors—white, heterosexual, (mostly) Christian men and

> women- are in constant battle with a number of "others": non-
> white races, Jews, homosexuals, etc.[165]

As an articulated form of dualism, binary discourse functions
to divide "white and black" along the dividing lines of perceived
virtues such as good and evil, American and un-American, righteous and corrupt, heroic and malicious, martyrs and murderers.
These were among some of the more common binaries drawn
from the hands of forum visitors and website members, and
crafted through some of the rhetorical patterns already examined
like socialized hate speech and message escalation. However,
whether divided along social grounds by a single voice, or parti-
tioned by the collective views of the responding masses, whites
and nonwhites are two entirely different *species* in the white power
domain.

As with other strategic mediated forms like newspapers editorials or political speeches, binary discourse is not an accidental
turn of the written word. Its deliberate design carries a specific
objective, such as to vilify a point of opposition, or heighten the
relevance of a cause, or simply to clarify the differences between
the two. However, presenting an idea or a people strictly as polar
opposites in any context is deceptive because it denies the actual
complexity and variety that exist in the real world. This is how
stereotypes are born, and later, reinforced. The Women for Aryan Unity website, for instance, has already established a strong
stereotype of the white Aryan female. In their own words, she is a
picture of "wisdom" and "honor," but most of all, "support" for
"building a...community for all our Aryan kin." However,
deeper within the growing Aryan community site, the dual nature of this matriarchal figure is further revealed:

> To be prepared for our future, the future of our men and chil-
> dren, is something white women should be thinking about and
> acting upon. There are various things that are necessary to

---

[165] Chip Berlet and Stanislav Vysotsky. "Overview of U.S. White Supremacists Groups." Journal of Political and Military Sociology. 34:1
(2006) 11-48

prepare ourselves for our fight against ZOG and other evils
that impose their destructive ways upon us…We must secure
the existence of our people and a future for White children.[166]

In this excerpt, the juxtaposition of two movements is presented clearly. On one side, Aryan women are depicted as preparing for the future of white men and children and securing
their existence. Yet, at the same time, the Zionist-Occupied
Government (Jews and their conspirators) are inflicting destructive measures upon that same Aryan existence. This is a classic
example of the nonwhite oppressor frame being employed in this
cyber-community to provoke a response, or in their words, "to
prepare ourselves for our fight."

Binary discourse in the white power forums is also designed
to suggest the underlying theme that a violent action is inevitable
between two opposing sides where one is presented as the oppressor, and the other, the oppressed. The ultra-vicious Podblanc
video sharing website was one of the community leaders in terms
of its public promotion of violent actions. Here, binary discourse
was spoken and even acted out in the video convergent media
format. Examples included uploaded videos like the "Suburban
Welcome Wagon for Inner City Guests," which portrayed a
white skinhead firing off a heavy artillery automatic rifle beneath
a written threat to illegal immigrants, or the much viewed "Nig-
gers, I hate you" tirade. This public video featured a young white
teenager speaking into his computer monitor spewing his opposition to black and Hispanic cultures before declaring, "You can
die."[167]

While the white power version of binary discourse could seldom be called subtle, occasional statements cleverly wove together two or more oppositional forces to present the idea of bi-
lateral and multilateral threats to the white community. The
Stormfront website, for instance, posted countless forums that

---

[166] Women for Aryan Unity. Retrieved August 24, 2009 from
http://wau14.com/
[167] Podblanc. "Video Uploads." Retrieved August 15, 2009 from
http://podblanc.com/

mirrored sentiments such as this one: "It's foolish to pick a side between Jews and Muslims, both must be viewed as an affront to European heritage and culture." Here, both Judaism and Islam are packaged together, as are many of the perceived enemies of white supremacists, which allow this racist community to present the *illusion* of a much larger and growing threat toward the new white minority.

However, not every example of oppositional discourse was crafted to vilify an entire religious people or collective racial threat. In fact, most forums seemed to center on smaller targets and individuals. On the New Saxon website, one member commented on Mark Potok, director of the Southern Poverty Law Center's Intelligence Project. They scorned, "I want to point out the fact that Potok made a comment about the great race war while insulting Rush and the right-wingers." Here, Potok, whose Intelligence Project shines a light on websites like the New Saxon, is placed in binary juxtaposition to rightwing radio host Rush Limbaugh. However, the New Saxon forum writer is merely using the perception of politics to express racism. He later continued, "[Potok] must see the turn in the political tide and the tsunami coming in the near future. This would not be a battle of Whites v. Blacks... It would be Whites against all natural enemies." In the end, the forum writer developed the binary of 'Potok versus Limbaugh' as a contextual means to tap into the more significant discourse of "Whites v. Blacks."

This same rhetorical strategy can be seen in another Stormfront forum, subheading titled, "Jew Axelrod Says 'Tea Party' Protesters Are 'Wrong'." Here, the vocal visitor asserts, "Mr. Axelrod is going to learn rather quickly what happens when civilians are forced by a tyranny to abandon their civilian status, and take control of themselves and their destiny." This ominous threat is no less aimed at "Jew Axelrod," the White House Chief Advisor, than it is at the White House itself. It is also an increasingly common example of the dangerous message alignment between anti-government and racist sentiments; message-types made notorious by the likes of Holocaust Museum shooter,

James von Brunn, and Oklahoma City bomber, Timothy McVeigh.

The focus on high profile violence was another popular topic of conversation among the more fanatical forums. On one end, nonwhite assailants, mostly black and Hispanic murderers, were regularly vilified by fellow site visitors. However, other killers like McVeigh, Von Brunn, Hitler, Eichmann, and Heydrich were frequently presented as the binary contrast to their nonwhite counterparts and often called "hero" and "martyr." One Hammerskin forum offered the following words on the annual 'Martyr's Day, December 8th,' "Let us all give thanks and respect to the brave that have stood their ground; for their blood, their race and their nation. We will never forget. 14 Words." Another inscriber later commented on "Jewish propaganda against one of our greatest heroes... Reinhard Heydrich, Jewkiller extraordinaire, possibly greatest man ever lived." The blatant lack of distinction between the terms villainous murderers and heroic martyrs is an alarming observation in this segment of white power culture. It reveals the extent to which the worst kind of violence is not only accepted by hate site visitors, but even glorified when malicious killers become revered like iconic rock stars of the community. The inherent danger in branding this kind of message to younger visitors, especially, is that impressionable minds will learn to fear the nonwhite threat, while at the same, idolize those heroic "martyrs" that bravely "stood their ground." Such leaders tend to inspire devoted followers.

Conclusion

By itself, white supremacy is merely an isolated and self-aggrandizing ideology. From the initial brochure of the homepage, qualities like social exclusivity and pride appear harmless and even appealing to some visitors. After all, everyday features like blogs, jokes, and chat rooms strongly resemble those typical online spaces frequented by many of today's college students. But a closer look at the inner-layer of these cyber dens tells a strikingly different story about the community. Deeper within the public forums and membership blogs, it becomes patently clear that white nationalism is no more isolated and harmless a movement than an idling tank.

In fact, true white supremacy, like the kind that is expressed within these leading websites, is far more concerned with external goals like publicity and racial uprising than just passively sponsoring a white identity. The proof of the white power movement's underlying fixation on "rahowa" – racial holy war – is evidenced in the printed words of their many devout members. The message of a white resistance shapes much of the local talk that invigorates website visitors with a communal sense that they are really David preparing to stand up to Goliath. It is that steady discourse of "us versus them," white against the rest, that strives to mobilize a younger online movement, whose net generational members are already suitably in their own process of development and search for identity.

In the culture of white power cyberspace, identity is regularly defined through patterned messages such as the ones we have examined. In this world, the common mind is one of binary vision, intent upon dividing issues, both big and small, into a basic class of white and nonwhite. Yet, the social acclimation process is not reserved entirely to the interests of race and identity, and perhaps, that is also strategically by design. Many website forums speak to familiar topics of American youth culture like sports, music, relationships, and school. These themes, dressed in social slang, are often the conversational bridges between the common banter of cyberspace and the foundations of hate speech. For this reason, website organizers have framed so many of their public forums behind subheadings like "music and entertainment" rather than their real subject matter, race and religion. However, the path to inflaming those and other provocative topics is not distant in the realm of the online forum where single phrases and codewords regularly trigger tirades that were likely waiting for their opportunity to surface.

Ultimately, cyberspace has made this public-based resurgence possible. The rhetorical trends of *message escalation* and *so-*

cialized hate speech are examples of *online* phenomena that thrive in the domain of white power websites. The popular forum provides the ideal structure for fostering sentiments which are not only interactive enough to inflame a public-driven debate, but also sufficiently anonymous so as to render an uninhibited flow of racism among like-minded visitors. It is this innermost space that reveals the deepest layer of white power discourse, and within which we find the truest face of these websites, finally unveiled and exposed.

7. Looking Ahead at the Minds and Message

For the average citizen not consumed with an agenda of racial superiority, there is little question as to whether websites like Stormfront or KKK.com ultimately promote hatred. Beneath the framed subtexts of white oppression and radical information lie the discernable messages of racism and anti-Semitism. But at the same time, a reality that cannot be overlooked is the sheer number of hate sites, which has increased by the *thousands* in the last five years, along with the consequential expansion of members and visitors to these online communities. And so, notwithstanding the better judgment of the average citizen, a new, highly vocal white power minority is nonetheless on the rise in America. In fact, by many new accounts, the amplification of hate speech is drawing cross-sectional support from a few mainstream sources like the political and youth culture bases.

While the growing white power minority is still just a fraction of the World Wide Web, the fact that they have built new inroads to the informational, political, and cultural arenas of cyberspace is no less significant a development. For every degree to which the dial of intolerance is moved closer to "normal," a higher tolerance for hate speech is established among the masses. The lines between political debate and hate speech slowly become increasingly ambiguous as the flow of information is diluted by racial undercurrents, and cultural stereotypes quietly become just another part of the American vernacular. In effect, by raising the bar of what qualifies as acceptable expressions of bigotry, we simultaneously lower the bar of civility and common sense in our culture.

On a more extreme level, however, the rising tide of cultural intolerance has also set a dangerous belief system in motion for a few violent radicals ardently devoted to the cause of white power hatred. As the white power movement has infiltrated Internet cultures and infected several conventional domains, its leading websites, such as Podblanc and the Creativity Alliance, have inspired the fringe segments of the community to interpret their motto of "racial holy war" at times, literally. As such, a final question still remains unanswered. How much responsibility should we assign to the online hate community with regard to the level of actual racial violence on our streets?

In an interview with U.S. News and World Report, Matt Hale contends that his group, the World Church of the Creator, "never incited violence."[168]

On July 4th weekend, two weeks prior to giving that statement, one of Matt Hale's closest followers went on a racial shooting spree. Benjamin N. Smith, a college sophomore who joined the group one year before, selectively shot eleven people; Blacks, Jews, and Asians. He murdered two people and wounded nine before killing himself. Smith was considered the prototypical recruit, "youthful and well educated." That vague criterion can describe just about any college student who surfs the web in search of a community to call their own. Yet, Matt Hale and the Creativity Alliance are not considered accomplices, in the legal sense, if one of their students decides to interpret the call for a white power uprising with violent expression.

Meanwhile, the legal debate over hate speech on the Internet continues as new hate websites emerge every year. The white power movement uses this debate to further its evidence-building case against those nameless conspirators who aim to oppress them. On a larger scale, however, the outspoken hate community is still largely confined to the limits of cyberspace. As vast as cyberspace may be, it still cannot substitute an actual community where outright racist activists are easily exposed, and violent acts are illegal. In 2005, Matt Hale was sentenced to 40 years in prison for soliciting the murder of a Jewish federal judge, Joan Lefkow.[169] The World Church of the Creator organization was

---

[168] Angie Cannon and Warren Cohen. "The Church of the Almighty White Man." U.S. News & World Report,   127:3 (1999).
[169] "Matt Hale." Retrieved October 27, 2009 from
http://www.adl.org/learn/ext_us/Hale.asp?LEARN_Cat=
Extremism&LEARN_SubCat=Extremism_in_America&
xpicked=2&item=mh (2007)

forced to relinquish its name due to a trademark lawsuit, the case over which Judge Lefkow was presiding. While Hale serves his sentence in the real world, the movement lives on in cyberspace where the World Church of the Creator has taken a new name, the Creativity Alliance.

As websites like creativityalliance.com continue to wire into the online infrastructure and establish new recruiting networks among the net generation, the political blogosphere, and the information bases, a new motto must underscore the road ahead for these and all other mediated platforms – Responsibility. More specifically, the new information age requires an updated and modified form of responsibility to counter these ever-adapting expressions of hate speech. In this sense, we are not just talking about a renewed focus on political correctness. After all, "political correctness" is merely a correction in language. In an unforeseen way, by removing the offensive language that surrounds race, gender, religion and sexuality from our culture, we have inadvertently silenced our ability to simply discuss our differences without the fear of offending someone. While the practice of political correctness has, at its base, good intentions, it is not a remedy for the actual illness of racial intolerance.

Instead of focusing on semantics in the new millennium, the next generation must move past language, and beyond politeness and passivity, to *counter-attack* hate speech where it lives. The vulnerable and sometimes even culpable sectors of the news media's political punditry, the popular information websites, and yes, the net generation themselves, must acknowledge a new kind of responsibility that comes with broadcasting and hosting public opinions in the cyber age. With specific regard to the recent advancements of the white power community and hate speech, this new vigilance will mean something different for these three sectors of media and culture: news and politics, online information, and the net generation. However, each of these actors will share the starring role in confronting social intolerance, and educating the community.

News and Politics

The news media has changed dramatically in the last 20 years. First, through the introduction of cable news, the 24-hour news cycle has gradually featured more national politics reporting, but also interjected a greater reliance on political commentaries to fill the daily programming. Today, news channels like CNN, Fox News, and MSNBC each represent not only a choice in televised news, but also a distinct political perspective and national opinion with which to associate one's self. In fact, it seems that in terms of politics, cable viewers no longer turn to Fox or CNN to get their daily news; instead, they are tuning in to acquire their daily views. However, this is nothing new. News and politics have long shared a symbiotic relationship throughout American history, as some of the earliest newspapers were much more partisan than they are today. As the news format has gradually evolved, so has the news product witnessed a shift in the flow of its reporting as well.

The second major change in the news media, which addresses more so the issue of social responsibility is the impact of the Internet and political blogoshere on the news and politics dynamic, and it is here where the white power movement has gained new ground. Whereas prior technological advancements in the media have always affected the news product, such as from print to radio, and radio to television, the Internet impact is different. Instead of transforming the style of the news product, as was the case with radio and television, the World Wide Web has actually altered the flow of information itself. The typical news gatekeepers have lost their absolute control of that flow as now, in cyberspace, news not only reaches the public audience but is also directly influenced and contributed to *by* them. Political blogs are a prime example of this reverse flow as they are public-driven editorials, many of which have also begun to receive larger followings than the newspaper opinion pages that are slowly disappearing in the electronic age. By way of the Internet, the news and opinion media are not only everywhere, but today they are also everyone.

In the theory of information laundering, this research demonstrated how the white power movement has tapped into the new wave of online blogs, news and politics, *from* which it has posted mainstream news stories onto hate website homepages in order to present the greater illusion of conventional support for its cause. Yet, we now know that hate speech and racism are not political causes in any sense, despite racial propagandists' savvy attempts to blur these two concepts into one. But amid the fire and smoke of today's real political scene, mainstream issues like diversity programs, immigration, gay marriage, and a growing criticism of a government led for the first time by a black president, each provide ideal and legitimate narratives upon which organized racists can pin their particular campaigns.

On the surface, narratives of racial hate disguised as politics appear legitimate, especially in web format. Some of the more common themes include a general push back against multicultural initiatives, the fear of losing traditional American values, and paranoia over the government and media's involvement in these alleged conspiracies. And, in many ways, all citizens have the right to express these kinds of concerns. However, the slippery slope begins at that point where the narrative shifts on a website like the Council of Conservative Citizens, from national concerns to insinuations of an unnamed entity behind the government, the media, and all of this change. In fact, that is how racial movements often begin, and political debates crossover into sinister questions that would normally never find expression in the mainstream press.

And so, we have come full circle, returning to the underlying issue of responsibility. In order to stop the funnel and flow of information laundering on the political news front, through which online racists are establishing a false backing and borrowed legitimacy, the news media themselves must consider how their words speak to *this* particular audience. While this may not be the intention of political pundits, and even politicians themselves, the reality is that their opinions on matters relating to various issues, particularly race or religion, are constantly being exploited by a growing hate movement in a manner quite different from their original meanings.

Today, a responsible news media outlet can combat the propagandist movement in three ways. First and foremost, they can return to a greater emphasis on news presentation and explanation of issues, rather than focusing so heavily as they now do on editorializing. While there may be entertainment value in that kind of news product increasingly found on the cable networks, more and more, issues like affirmative action and immigration are being cut by news analysts into two sides – right and left – and this only simplifies what are complex issues along the same political narrative. However, for groups like the white power movement, which already think in absolutes and speak in binary terms, this type of polarized news reporting actually promotes "sides" in America, which in turn, caters directly to the white nationalist belief system.

Second, and more importantly, news outlets must become more vigilant about what they say when their broadcasters or guest pundits do editorialize about heated social issues. One of the most pressing examples of the need for greater caution in reporting is the coverage of antigovernment sentiment across the country. One need only recall the Civil Rights era or the 1970s antiwar protests to acknowledge how easily healthy expressions of government protest can become inflamed and, sometimes, violent. Today more than ever, the news media that covers antigovernment demonstrations must understand that, while all public debate is protected, racial radicalism is dangerously on the rise within these same venues. In May, 2009, the Anti-Defamation League (ADL) reported how white supremacist groups were using the 'Tea Party' antigovernment platform "to disseminate their hateful views and recruit a larger following."[170] Just as this research has done, the ADL report went directly to the source for evidence, providing telling excerpts from the Stormfront website

---

[170] "White Supremacists and Anti-Semites Plan to Recruit at July 4 Tea Parties." Retrieved October 1, 2009 from http://www.adl.org/ main_Extremism/White_Supremacists_July_4_Tea_Parties.htm

forums. Among the posts they cited, one encouraged the immediate community to, "Take these Tea Party Americans by the
hand and help them go from crawling to standing independently
and then walking toward racialism." Another post declared, "A
big crowd of irate White folks protesting the government seems
like the perfect time and place for us WN's (White Nationalists)
to promote our cause." And yet another respondent agreed, "I
think they'd be ideal for spreading WN literature and gaining
recruits in large numbers, more quickly."

In addition to white nationalist infiltrations into the public
demonstration scene, there has also been noted increase in activity among rightwing militias since the 2008 presidential election.
A 2009 Southern Poverty Law Center report on the "Return of
the Militias" in America shines a spotlight on the recent convergence of racial hate and political anger among this society. "The
situation has many authorities worried. Militia men, white supremacists, anti-Semites, nativists, tax protesters and a range of
other protesters of the radical right are cross-pollinating and may
even be coalescing." [171] The same report went on to attribute
some of the rise in antigovernment sentiment to conventional
sources like a U.S. Representative that "warned of 17 'socialists'
in Congress," ala Joseph McCarthy, or a Fox News host that has
called "[President] Obama a fascist, a Nazi and a Marxist." Such
forms of news and politics have not only been welcomingly embraced by the white power community, but also posted as eye-
catching headlines on their homepages.

Finally, in addition to being more mindful about the way the
press covers heated issues, like public protests or immigration,
these same media giants must also become vigilant about who
their network, newspaper, or webpage hosts. Perhaps, the greatest victory for the white power movement, or any extremist organization, is publicity. It is for this reason that groups like the
Westboro Baptist Church send out press releases before arriving
on a local scene with their "God Hates Fags" signs, and websites

---

[171] Larry Keller. "Return of the Militias." Retrieved October 10, 2009
from http://www.splcenter.org/news/item.jsp?pid=415

like KKK.com instruct visitors how to contact their local governments and press offices. The news media, as well as prominent political figures, sometimes fall into the trap of hosting extremist representatives to discuss mainstream matters, but in effect, what they have really done is help validate the radical causes for which they stand.

Other times, the media outlet itself is to blame for foolishly sponsoring outright stereotypes. The Southern Poverty Law Center asserts, "Respectable news organizations should not be peddling propaganda that supports the agenda of radical extremists who are only interested in stirring up hate and fomenting violence."[172] But as recently as October, 2009, the popular South Carolina newspaper, *The Times and Democrat,* printed an opinion piece written by two GOP chairmen on the subject of congressional earmarks. The republican state leaders wrote, "There is a saying that the Jews who are wealthy got that way not by watching dollars, but instead by taking care of the pennies and the dollars taking care of themselves."[173] While the two chairmen later apologized for the remark, it took little time for this anti-Semitic comment to surface on leading white power websites. Of course, one is left to wonder why *The Times and Democrat* would print such an op-ed in the first place. Or, for that matter, why cable news networks continue to cover the "Obama birther movement" despite that story's apparent incredulities and white power origins.

Does race sell? Certainly within American culture, race and diversity are commonplace issues, so there is a logical public interest in having news and opinions presented on these matters. But what about racism, or the issue of multicultural expansion in the United States? Did Fox News host, Glenn Beck, pique an audience's interest when he discussed the possibility of Mexico

---

[172] Richard Cohen. "SPLC President Calls on CNN to Remove Lou Dobbs from Air." Retrieved October 9, 2009 from http://www.splcenter.org/news/item.jsp?aid=390
[173] "Republican chairmen apologize for Jew remark." Retrieved October 22, 2009 fromhttp://www.msnbc.msn.com/id/33406727/ns/politics-more_politics/

collapsing: "Does anyone think there will be a rush of people…they're going to reclaim California? That they're going to
reclaim Texas?"[174] Did MSNBC's *Meet the Press* draw higher ratings by giving airtime to a racist provocateur like Louis Farrakhan who said on that program, "They [the Jews] are the greatest controllers of Black minds, Black intelligence"[175] Do anti-
Semitic and anti-Islamic quotes sell more books when conservative writer, Ann Coulter, tells TV viewers that 'Jews are people
who need to be "perfected" and Muslims are "ragheads"?[176] If
the answers to all of these questions are "yes," then reexamining
the media's ability to stoke racial fears for ratings must also take
into account their audience – the American people – who continue coming back for more. Certainly, not every media outlet
that discusses racial issues or hosts anti-Semitic speakers is, therefore, a beacon for bigotry. These *are* important public matters to
address. But with the knowledge that white power fanatics are
beginning to draw racist sentiments and followers from the same
well as political analysts and news personalities, these mainstream voices of information now have an equally important role
to become a mainstream voice of reason.

Online Information

According to Schweitzer's 2008 study, "a majority of first-
year college students referred to Wikipedia at least once for a
high school paper, and nearly 80% of advanced college students

---

[174] "Hate in the mainstream: Quotes from the right." Retrieved October 9, 2009 from
http://www.splcenter.org/intel/intelreport/article.jsp?aid=1054
[175] "Farrakhan in his own words." Retrieved October 9, 2009 from
http://www.adl.org/special_reports/farrakhan_own_words2/on_jews.asp
[176] "Hate in the Mainstream: Ann Coulter Defends White Supremacist
Group." Retrieved October 10, 2009 from
http://www.splcenter.org/intel/intelreport/article.jsp?aid=1048

did so for their college papers."[177] While Wikipedia is the most popular research tool on the web, and often a very useful one at that, there is no disputing whether or not this website occasionally offers inaccurate information. As a public-driven website that is open to the masses, the "collective nature" of Wikipedia makes the online encyclopedia prone to inaccuracies, exaggeration, and sometimes, even fabrications. In terms of cyber information, Wikipedia is an excellent example of a research base with good intentions and academic objectives, but at the same time, it is also a perfect entrance point for anyone with less-than-honorable purpose.

Online information itself represents the next evolution in an educational tool. However, a greater responsibility must also be assigned to this new public sphere of worldwide scholarship that offers more access, but provides fewer gatekeepers monitoring the quality and nature of the input. That is what makes online information bases such prime real estate for groups like the Supreme White Alliance or Stormfront. Like news and political blogs, online information spaces act as both a conduit to white power websites, and an involuntary filter for their laundered form of information. In the world of scholars, librarians, and information specialists, there is no greater enemy to enlightenment than falsified-knowledge, and racist propaganda certainly qualifies as that. To counter its dissemination in the wide open realm of cyberspace, online information bases must both defend and fortify their intellectual grounds upon two fronts.

First, both the information websites *and* their hosting networks have to become more accountable and aware of the day-to-day material they house and publish. Who is utilizing these open websites? How is the information space being used, or more aptly, misused if that is the case? Websites, like network hosts, are private entities and, as such, they have both the right and responsibility to deny their platforms to those that use them to express

---

[177] Nick J. Schweitzer. "Wikipedia and Psychology: Coverage of Concepts and Its Use by Undergraduate Students." Teaching of Psychology, 35 (2008) 81-85.

hate speech. In this way, online information providers must treat their websites like open fields that regularly require surveying eyes, and occasionally, pulling up the weeds that have moved in from underground. This weeding process should be a public one, so that when a website like American Renaissance posts anti-Hispanic material onto an information site about immigration, that website can inform the community of its removal, but more importantly, the reason for it.

Outspoken vigilance against online hate speech is not only an aggressive approach to counter widespread extremism; it is also a needed, modernized tool of education that will teach users about the pitfalls in the terrain of cyberspace. That is why the second front of intellectual defense are the online watchdog organizations that volunteer their efforts to be both a trail guide pointing out the perils of the online environment, while simultaneously acting as an educator with regard to intolerance in our culture. In this text, we have turned to the work of several of these watchdog educators, whose websites and literature have helped to identify thousands of hate websites, decode their language, and monitor the extremists and their trends. In relation to the white power websites, these watchdog sites live at the opposite end of the spectrum of the online democratic sphere. Social community organizations like the Anti-Defamation League, Southern Poverty Law Center, Simon Wiesenthal Center, National Association for the Advancement of Colored People, National Council of La Raza, and the Gay & Lesbian Alliance Against Defamation, have each built websites of their own to monitor and report hate group activities on the web, and in public life, in order to protect their cultural communities. These groups speak to the counteractive civic potential of the World Wide Web in exposing hate-based websites for what they actually are by also confronting issues behind online hate.

The work of an anti-hate organization is not easy, especially in cyberspace where there is little if any legal oversight, and the white power movement is working just as hard to blend in with the rest of the digital landscape. But organizations like the Anti-Defamation League have taken an important step back in order to see the forest for the trees. The ADL is well aware of the Internet's new potential for allowing anti-Semites and racists to come together and recruit others. As both a watchdog and an educator, their group exposes the racist agenda of the white power movement, while also releasing an annual report on hate group activity across the globe. In addition, the ADL also works with federal law enforcement agencies to locate potential Benjamin Smiths before they strike. The Simon Wiesenthal Center is another organization dedicated to fighting online bigotry. The Center has built museums dedicated to teaching tolerance while annually reporting on *Digital Terrorism and Hate.* That report focuses on thousands of hate-based websites and is distributed yearly to "government agencies, community activists, educators, and members of the media."[178] Private organizations like these represent the power of citizen-based groups to use *anti*-hate speech measures and *factual* online information as the best weapons against social intolerance.

One of the primary ways that these monitors of online information counter hate speech is by making public statements opposing mainstream trends toward intolerance, such as incidents of racial stereotyping. These denouncements are often made more for the sake of educating the greater community than they are for vilifying select members. For example, in October, 2009, the ADL responded on its website to a "prominent Christian religious leader...for comparing proposed healthcare reform measures to 'what the Nazis did' and for bestowing a Josef Mengele Award on the president's chief healthcare advisor."[179] Using this extreme analogy as an opportunity to educate, ADL chairman Abraham Foxman publicly explained why such comparisons are "offensive and diminish the history and memory" of those 11 million murdered at the hands of the Nazis: "We hope

---

[178] Southern Poverty Law Center. "About Us." Retrieved October 8, 2009 from http://www.splcenter.org/center/about.jsp

[179] "ADL Welcomes Christian Leader's Apology For Insensitive Remarks On Healthcare Debate." Retrieved October 20, 2009 from http://www.adl.org/PresRele/ChJew_31/5623_31.html

that this episode will serve as a teachable moment that will help
to improve understanding about Jewish history, anti-Semitism
and the Holocaust, and that the use of Nazi analogies will cease."
The President of the Southern Baptist Ethics and Religious Liberty Commission, who made the analogy, apologized sincerely
for equating "anyone in the Obama administration with Dr.
Mengele."

Beyond these teachable moments, the educational community as a whole can do more to confront the issues of social intolerance and hate speech in cyberspace. The growing existence of
these bigoted belief systems and online contaminants of information calls for a new mandatory form of education about encoun-
tering racism in the new media landscape. The scholars of both
media and information studies must develop new programs that
teach young adults to become active examiners of their mass
communications intake, especially on the Internet. A modernized
focus on media literacy and information systems can instruct Internet-users on the differences between political debates and hate
speech, or race-based information and racist propaganda, while
starting an open and healthy discussion with students about cyberspace itself. In some sectors of education, this dialogue has
already begun, but its chief communicators must begin to play a
more active and participatory role in the process. We are, of
course, talking about the last piece of this equation, the net generation.

The Net Generation

In cyberspace, all the elements of media that we have covered in this book – the white power websites, the watchdog organizations, political blogosphere, information spaces, and social
networking sites – have each built an agenda for reaching the net
generation. In the future, every one of these special interests will
need this next generation that were born into the Internet, to
become their chief spokesmen, members, customers, leaders,
voters, and students within that same virtual space. And as this
country continues to diversify demographically, it is the mind

and message of the net generation for whom groups like White
Aryan Resistance (WAR) and the Anti-Defamation League will
be competing. Given the high stakes nature of this massive advertising campaign, it goes without question that the greatest
amount of social responsibility lay in the very hands of the target
audience of all these organizations, websites, and movements.

The net generation stands at the epicenter of a turbulent and
changing world. And in the present evolution of global mass
communication, they are the constant recipients of an awesome
amount of digital information zooming in and out of their lives
like nonstop traffic. It is only fair to stop and recognize the
heightened challenge they face in addressing the questions and
decisions that this age has put before them. "Is my identity a
race, religion, or nationality, or is it simply the color of my skin –
the box I check off on a form? What if I am all these things?
With whom then do I associate? What about the Internet? Are
all of these online communities part of the 'real world'? Am I
talking with a friend in this chat room – or to a stranger? Do I
trust this information?" In fact, if the younger generation is pon-
dering questions like these in the future, regardless of the answers
they are already taking an important step towards becoming socially responsible citizens. They are surveying the waters before
diving in headfirst.

In addition to introspection, and maintaining a responsible
internal dialogue, the net generation will also be accountable to
the outside elements, and engaging that conversation with their
teachers about new media literacy and information systems.
With their unique and firsthand perspectives, kids from the ages
of 10 to 25 can be both the students and the educators of topics
like safely navigating through the online universe, identifying
hate speech in cyberspace, recognizing trusted information, and
rejecting propaganda. Online, they can also participate in the
new *civic journalism,* in which news and opinions are provided by
everyday citizens with an underlying focus on how these facts or
issues affect the immediate or greater community. The Pew Center for Civic Journalism conducts regular research on how this
mass communicative trend, driven largely by increased Internet

activity and access, helps to "empower a community" through a more public media system that watches over one another.[180]

In terms of the growing movement of white power extremism and online recruitment, civic journalism can inform the youth culture, in particular, whenever their popular spaces have been breached by inscribers of intolerance. On a similar note, social networking websites, such as Facebook and Twitter, must promote higher community standards and social responsibilities in their own domains which are both powered and occupied by the net generation. The same is true for other mainstream adolescent sites like YouTube, Flickr, MySpace, Bebo, and College-Humor, which in many ways, have obscured the notion of a youth culture behind private screen names and online personas. Whereas in the past, adolescents were identifying solely with local subcultures and trends like punk rock and gangster styles, today much of their identities are being constructed in cyberspace. For the white power movement, this new setting for adolescent development has meant an opportunistic shift in the kinds of kids they are able recruit.

In past years, according to Dobratz and Waldner (2006), youth subcultures that usually identified with the white power typology were "black metal supporters, and fans of a number of musical styles that broadly fall under the catchall labels of industrial/noise, apocalyptic folk, and gothic."[181] While these often outcast segments of the young social scene are still among those prone to an anti-establishment message, and empowered by ideas like white supremacy, the World Wide Web has given these ideologies a much larger and conventional pool of applicants from which to choose. With that being the case, the net generation must equip themselves with the new awareness that many websites *are not* what they appear to be. Despite their familiarity

---

[180] Pew Center for Civic Journalism. Retrieved October 12, 2009, from http://www.pewcenter.org/

[181] Betty A. Dobratz and Lisa K. Waldner. "In Search of Understanding the White Power Movement." Journal of Political and Military Sociology, 34:1 (2006) 2.

in form and function – the games they offer, or clubs they promote, and information tools that they provide – these websites
represent the classic bait and switch model. Instead of the promise of friendship, allure of entertainment, or the pledge of legitimate information, the white power website, in its actual form,
delivers a sophisticated recruitment center for nurturing hatred.

As the new prospect steadily becomes indoctrinated into
these pseudo-informational and cultural web communities, the
interconnected online environment ultimately leads back into the
concrete world where we began our investigation. Berlet and
Vysotsky (2006) describe the typical pattern of youth recruitment
that follows the online initiation phase. They write:

> Rock concerts, parties, and subcultural..."hangouts" are loca-
> tions where new recruits are exposed to the politics of white
> supremacy and the subculture of the movement. Older mem-
> bers (who are respected by all the members of the subculture,
> new and old alike) reinforce the ideals and norms in these set-
> tings.[182]

For the young recruit, they are filled with a new sense of
value, self-importance, and belonging by community elders and
their new friends. They also begin to see "differences" in the
world around them which they had never noticed before, such as
the way one race acts inferiorly to another, or how a "nonwhite"
religion undermines the white, Christian society. This is the belief system that racist propagandists are producing, packaging
and selling to any white member of the net generation, but most
desirably, to the angry and the naive.

In addition to asking questions and promoting awareness
about the nature of media and information in cyberspace, a socially responsible net generation must acquire a mature understanding about the sinister elements that purvey that world, and
where they lead. Teaching about intolerance and racism is no

---

[182] Chip Berlet and Stanislav Vysotsky. "Overview of U.S. White Supremacists Groups." *Journal of Political and Military Sociology. 34:1* (2006)
30-32.

easy task, especially to a young audience that has been inundated with lessons of equality and multiculturalism since grade school. Such themes can begin to seem tiresome and dull when they will matter most, during the period of teenage exploration and development. Growing up during these times means understanding that access to online information is actually not free. Rather, it is a privilege that comes with the price of responsibility and maturity, and, like any trial of young adulthood, a true test of character.

Conclusion – The White Power Movement

So what does the future hold for the white power movement in cyberspace? While watchdog groups actively work to identify and expose these "user-friendly" communities for what they are, it appears from this research that white power movement websites are continuing to adapt to the new media. The links to YouTube and Facebook signify a movement that is keeping up with the times. The convergence of text, audio, and video on almost all of the leading websites demonstrate the high-tech capabilities of these sites necessary for attracting younger, net-savvy audiences. The branding of hate symbols onto stickers and jackets, as well as the sales of white power music and clothing suggest an overall culture which the white power movement is attempting to market online. The international networking component of these websites further suggests intentions to grow the cause into a worldwide movement.

From these findings, one might conclude that the white power movement's adaptation into cyberspace has been a success. However, only time will tell the extent to which the success of this virtual community will manifest itself into success in the actual world where the public resides. Future studies might attempt to link the online activities of groups like the Hammerskin Nation and the White Boy Society with the physical results they produce in society. For instance, a quantitative analysis of signifiers such as local chapter memberships, political representation, and college-based organizations could provide further evidence of the white power movement's advancements beyond the cyber platform. Regardless of their expansion, there still remains one simple truth about legally-protected, online hate speech. "Hate speech uncovers the haters."[183]

By drawing back their own curtain, the white power community, through its online operation, real-time dialogues, and self-evident strategy have revealed themselves to the world. Hence, another reason for their desire to hide behind artificial window dressings like information databases, news bulletins, and children's video games. Unveiled, these modern forms of media are simply the age-old expressions of intolerance, hostility, and, in truth, ignorance. Outside of cyberspace and back in the real world, however, the white power movement that claims to be the victim of a nonwhite majority *is* right about one thing. They are a minority. As an imaginary league of underdogs, they are victims of their own warped mentality. But not the mentality of self-perceived greatness or even the delusions of grandeur, because white power, like any social hate system, actually has little to do with cultural supremacy. Rather, these are the products of an individual's conceived smallness in society, and the white power movement is the cultivated response to that condition, but a dangerous one.

The first step in eradicating such threats to society is recognizing them. By illuminating the ugly truth hidden within the slick cyber dens of these 26 white power websites, we can isolate and expose the presence of hate on the Internet. In the new public sphere and marketplace of ideas that has come to be called "the information superhighway," these racist databases and social hate networks are the insidious hitchhikers that we must avoid trusting, despite the apparent sincerity of their appeal. Beneath the allure of the message and flash of its presentation, the new racial propaganda is like any other bad piece of information.

---

[183] Paul K. McMasters. "Must a Civil Society Be a Censored Society?" Human Rights: Journal of the Section of Individual Rights & Responsibilities, 26:4 (1999).

Once recognized, the next sensible move is to crumple it up and throw it away.

Bibliography

About the KKK (2009). Retrieved June 21, 2009, from
http://www.adl.org/learn/ext_us/kkk/default.asp?LEA
RN_Cat=Extremism&LEARN_SubCat=Extremism_in
_America&xpicked=4&item=kkk

Active U.S. Hate Groups in 2008: Neo-Nazi (2009). Retrieved
June 28, 2009, from
http://www.splcenter.org/intel/map/type.jsp?DT=9.

Adams, J., & Roscigno, V.J. (2005). White supremacists, oppositional culture and the World Wide Web. *Social Forces,
84:2*, 759-777.

ADL Welcomes Christian Leader's Apology For Insensitive Remarks On Healthcare Debate (2009). Retrieved October
20, 2009 from http://www.adl.org/PresRele/
ChJew_31/5623_31.htmC

Akdeniz, Y. (2002). Anonymity, democracy, and cyberspace. *Social Research, 69:1.*

Alexa web information company (2009). Retrieved on August 20,
2009, from http://alexa.com/.

Alexa Web Information: Facebook (2009). Retrieved on August
3, 2009, from http://alexa.com/siteinfo/facebook.com

Alexa web information company: Institute for Historical Review
(2009).Retrieved on June 28, 2009, from
http://alexa.com/siteinfo/ihr.org

Anti-Defamation League (2001). *Poisoning the web: Hatred online.*
New York: An ADL Publication.

Aryan Encyclopedia Takes Off (2007). Retrieved on June 20,
2009, from http://www.splcenter.org/intel/
intelreport/article.jsp?aid=863

Aryanwear (2009). Retrieved on September 1, 2009, from
    http://aryanwear.com/

Ask search: Holocaust (2009). Retrieved on August 20, 2009,
    from http://www.ask.com/web?q=Holocaust
    &qsrc=0&frstpgo=0&o=0&l=dir&qid=97C2C68CC46
    ADFACE2E38AC40D32A2CA&page=3&jss=1

Bandura, A. (1962). Social learning through imitation. In M.R.
    Jones (Ed.), *Nebraska symposium on motivation* (Vol. 10). Lin-
    coln: University of Nebraska Press.

Banschick, M.R., & Banschick, J.S. (2003). Children in cyber-
    space. In Leonard Shyles' (Ed.) *Deciphering Cyberspace:
    Making the Most of Digital Communication Technology.* Thou-
    sand Oaks, CA: Sage Publications, 159-199.

Bazyler, M.J. (2006). Holocaust denial laws and other legislation
    criminalizing promotion of Nazism. Retrieved August, 1,
    2009, from http://www1.yadvashem.org/
    about_yad/departments/audio/Bazyler.pdf

Becker, P.J., Byers, B., & Jipson, A. (2000). The contentious
    American debate: The first amendment and Internet-
    based hate speech. *International Review of Law Computers,
    14:1.*

Behind the Gunfire (2009). Alleged murderer inspired by pod-
    blanc website. Retrieved on June 23, 2009, from
    http://www.splcenter.org/intel/intelreport/article.jsp?ai
    d=1065

Beirich, H., & Moser, B. (2004). Communing with the council.
    Retrieved June 20, 2009, from
    http://www.splcenter.org/intel/intelreport/article.jsp?ai
    d=487

Berlet, C., & Vysotsky, S. (2006). Overview of U.S. white su-
    premacists groups. *Journal of Political and Military Sociology,
    34:1,* 30-32.

Bing search: Islamic (2009). Retrieved on August 20, 2009, from http://www.bing.com/search?q=Islam&first=21&FOR M=PERE1

Borrowman, S. (1999). Critical surfing: Holocaust deniability and credibility on the web. *College Teaching, 47:2*, 44-54.

Cannon, A., & Cohen, W. (1999). The church of the almighty white man. *U.S. News & World Report, 127:3*.

Charles Darwin Research Institute (2009). Retrieved September 10, 2009 from http://www.charlesdarwinresearch.org/

Cialdini, R.B., Bassett, R., & Cacioppo, J.T. (1978). Low-ball procedure for producing compliance. *Journal of Personality and Social Psychology, 36:5*, 463-76.

Cohen, A. (2003). White power music is an effective recruiting tool. In *White Supremacy Groups,* Farmington Hills, MI: Greenhaven Press.

Cohen, R. (2009). SPLC president calls on CNN to remove Lou Dobbs from air. Retrieved October 9, 2009, from http://www.splcenter.org/news/item.jsp?aid=390

Coe, K., Domke, D., Graham, E.S., John, S.L., & Pickard, V.W. (2004). No shades of gray: The binary discourse of George W. Bush and an echoing press. *Journal of Communication, 54:2*, 334-252.

Council of Conservative Citizens (2009). Retrieved on June 22, 2009, from http://cofcc.org/

Creativity Alliance (2009). Retrieved August 20, 2009 from http://www.creativityalliance.com/index.html

Creativity Alliance (2009). Mission statement. Retrieved on September 10, 2009 from http://www.creativityalliance.com/index.html

Creativity Alliance (2009). Video downloads. Retrieved September 10, 2009 from
http://www.creativityalliance.com/video.htm

David Duke. Retrieved from the Anti-Defamation League website on August 1, 2009, from
http://www.adl.org/learn/ext_us/
david_duke/default.asp.

Dijk, J. van (2005). *The network society: Social aspects of new media.* Thousand Oaks, CA: Sage Publications, Second Edition.

Dobratz, B.A., & Waldner, L.K. (2006). Search of understanding the white power movement. *Journal of Political and Military Sociology, 34:1.*

Doig, W. (2008). Homophobosphere. *The Advocate, 1002.* Retrieved on August 1, 2009, from
http://www.advocate.com/issue_story_ektid51690.asp

Don Black: White Pride World Wide (2009). Retrieved on June 19, 2009, from
http://www.adl.org/poisoning_web/black.asp

Dornberg, J. (1982). *Munich 1923: The story of Hitler's first grab for power.* New York, NY: Harper & Row, Publishers, 49-55.

Einzinger, K. (2009). Media regulation on the Internet. In "Hate Speech on the Internet." Retrieved August 1, 2009, from
http://www.osce.org/publications/rfm/2004/12/12239
_94_en.pdf, 142-149.

Eisner, W. (2005). *The plot: The secret story of the protocols of the elders of Zion.* New York: W.W. Norton & Company.

Emery, T., & Robbins, L. (2009). Holocaust museum shooter James von Brunn had history of hate. Retrieved July 20, 2009, from http://seattletimes.nwsource.com/html/
nationworld/2009330156_holocaustshooting12.html

Entman, R.M. (1993). Framing: Towards clarification of a fractured paradigm. *Journal of Communication, 43,* 51-58.

Extremism in the Media. (2009). Retrieved on August 20, 2009,
     from http://www.splcenter.org/intel/intelreport/
     article.jsp?aid=1007

Family Research Institute (2009). Retrieved August 28, 2009
     http://www.familyresearchinst.org/

Family Research Institute (2009). Scientific articles. Retrieved on
     September 10, 2009 from
     http://www.familyresearchinst.org/category/articles/

Farrakhan in his own words (2009). Retrieved October 9, 2009,
     from http://www.adl.org/special_reports/
     farrakhan_own_words2/on_jews.asp

FBI: Incidents and Offenses (2009). Retrieved July 20, 2009,
     from http://www.fbi.gov/ucr/hc2007/incidents.htm

FBI: Murder, Violent Crime Drop in 2008 (2009). Retrieved
     September 12, 2009 from http://www.cbsnews.com/
     stories/2009/09/14/national/main5309836.shtm

Fears, D., & Fisher, M. (2009). A suspect's long history of hate,
     and signs of strain. Retrieved July 20, 2009, from
     http://www.washingtonpost.com/wp-dyn/content/ ar-
     ticle/2009/06/10/AR2009061003495.html?
     sid=ST2009061200050

Final Solution (2009). Retrieved September 12, 2009 from
     http://www.finalsolution88.com/

Games Extremists Play (2002). Retrieved on September 1, 2009,
     from http://www.splcenter.org/intel/intelreport/
     article.jsp?aid=124

Gardner, R. (2000). Is AOL worse than TV? *New York Magazine.*

Gilgoff, D. (2009). Rev. Jeremiah Wright says Jews are prevent-
     ing Obama from talking to him. Retrieved September 4,
     2009 from http://www.usnews.com/blogs/god-and-
     country/2009/06/11/rev-jeremiah-wright-says-jews-
     are-preventing-obama-from-talking-to-him.html

God hates fags (2009). Retrieved on June 20, 2009, from
    http://www.godhatesfags.com/.

God hates fags (2009). Marine funeral picketing event. Retrieved
    September 5, 2009 from http://www.godhatesfags.com/

Goffman, E. (1974). *Frame analysis: An essay on the organizational of
    experience.* London: Harper and Row.

Google search: Black People (2009) Retrieved on August 20,
    2009 from http://www.google.com/search?
    sourceid=navclient&ie=UTF8&rlz=1T4RNWI_en
    US280US280&q=black+people

Google search: White People (2009). Retrieved on August 20,
    2009, from http://www.google.com/search?hl=en&
    source=hp&q=black+people&aq=f&oq=&aqi=g-z1g9

Graham, N. (2009). Rush Limbaugh – Obama's America. Re-
    trieved September 16, 2009 from
    http://www.huffingtonpost.com/2009/09/16/rush-
    limbaugh-obamas-amer_n_288371.html

Hammerskin Forums: General Discussion Area (2009). Retrieved
    September 17, 2009 from
    http://hammerskins.net/forum/index.php/topic,2289.
    msg21191.html#msg21191

Hate in the Mainstream: Ann Coulter Defends White Suprema-
    cist Group (2009). Retrieved October 10, 2009, from
    http://www.splcenter.org/intel/intelreport/article.jsp?ai
    d=1048

Hate in the mainstream: Quotes from the right. (2009). Re-
    trieved October 9, 2009, from
    http://www.splcenter.org/intel/intelreport/article.jsp?ai
    d=1054

Hate Symbols (2009). Retrieved August 22, 2009 from
    http://www.adl.org/hate_symbols/default.asp

Herbeck, D. (2003). Chaplinsky v. New Hampshire. In Richard
    Parker's (ed.) *Free Speech on Trial: Communication Perspectives
    on Landmark Supreme Court Decisions.* Tuscaloosa, AL: Uni-
    versity of Alabama Press.

Herf, J. (2006). *The Jewish enemy: Nazi propaganda during World War
    II and the Holocaust.* Cambridge, MA: The Belknap Press
    of Harvard University press.

Herman, E, & Chomsky, N. (2002). *Manufacturing consent: The po-
    litical economy of the mass media.* New York: Pantheon
    Books, a division of Random House, Inc.

Institute for Historical Review (2009). Library & archives. Re-
    trieved September 4, 2009 from
    http://www.ihr.org/main/library.shtml

Jews Destroyer of Cultures (2009). Retrieved September 17,
    2009 from http://hammerskins.net/forum/
    index.php/topic,235.0.html

Jewwatch homepage (2009). Retrieved September 3, 2009 from
    http://jewwatch.com/ homepage

Johnson-Cartee, K.S., & Copeland, G. (2003). *Strategic political
    communication: Rethinking social influence, persuasion, and propa-
    ganda.* Lanham, MD: Rowman & Littlefield Publishers.

Jowett, G.S., & O'Donnell, V. (1999). *Propaganda and persuasion.*
    Thousand Oaks, California: SAGE Publications.

Jowett, G.S., & O'Donnell, V. (2005). *Readings in propaganda and
    persuasion: New and classic essays.* Thousand Oaks, Califor-
    nia: SAGE Publications.

Institute for Historical Review: Outlet for Denial Propaganda
    (2009). Retrieved on June 21, 2009,
    fromhttp://www.adl.org/holocaust/ihr.asp

Keller, L. (2009). Return of the militias. Retrieved October 10,
    2009, from
    http://www.splcenter.org/news/item.jsp?pid=415

Klein, A. Byerly, C., & McEachern, T. (2009). Counterframing public dissent: U.S. coverage of the Iraq antiwar movement. *Critical Studies in Media Communication, 26:4,* 331-350.

KKK homepage (2009). Retrieved September 10, 2009 from http://www.kkk.com/

Knights Party Youth Corp (2009). Retrieved September 4, 2009 from http://www.kkk.bz/youthcorp.htm

Kreimer, S.F. (2001). Technologies of protest: Insurgent social movements and the first amendment in the era of the Internet. *University of Pennsylvania Law Review, 150:1.*

Ku Klux Klan (2009). Our goal. Retrieved September 8, 2009 from http://www.kkk.bz/ourgoal.htm

Laramie Project Rallies (2009). Retrieved on September 12, 2009 from http://www.godhatesfags.com/written/fliers/20091003_Laramie-Project-Boston-MA-Philadelphia-PA-and-Reston-VA.pdf

Lee, A.C., & Lee, E.B. (1939). *The fine art of propaganda.* New York: Harcourt, Brace and Co., Inc.

Lester, J., & Koehler, Jr., W.C. (2003). *Fundamentals of information studies: Understanding information and its environment.* New York: Neal-Schuman Publishers, Inc.

Leung, L. (2004). Net-generation attributes and seductive properties of the Internet as predictors of online activities and Internet addiction. *CyberPsychology & Behavior, 7:3.*

Lewandowski, D. (2008). Search engine user behavior: How can users be guided to quality content? *Information Services & Use, 28,* 261-268.

Loeb, H.A. (1999). Words have consequences: Reframing the hate speech debate. *Human Rights: Journal of the Section of Individual Rights & Responsibilities, 26:4.*

MacMillan, D. (2009). Facebook's Holocaust controversy. Retrieved August 3, 2009, from http://www.businessweek.com/technology/content/may2009/tc20090512_104433.htm

Magdoff, J., & Rubin, J.B. (2003). Social and psychological uses of the Internet. In Leonard Shyles' (Ed.) *Deciphering Cyberspace: Making the Most of Digital Communication Technology.* Thousand Oaks, CA: Sage Publications, 201-216.

Matt Hale (2007). Retrieved October 27, 2007, from http://www.adl.org/learn/ext_us/Hale.asp?LEARN_Cat=Extremism&LEARN_SubCat=Extremism_in_America&xpicked=2&item=mh

McAlister, A. (2009). Teaching the millennial generation. *American Music Teacher, 58:7.*

McCombs, M.E., & Shaw D.L. (1972) The agenda-setting function of mass media. *Public Opinion Quarterly, 36,* 176-187.

McLuhan, M. (1964). *Understanding media: The extensions of man.* Cambridge, MA: MIT Press.

McMasters, P.K. (1999). Must a civil society be a censored society? *Human Rights:* Journal of the Section of Individual Rights & Responsibilities, 26:4.

Meek, J.G., & Schapiro, R. (2009). Holocaust museum shooter. Retrieved July 20, 2009, from http://www.nydailynews.com/news/us_world/2009/06/10/2009-06-10_holocaust_museum_shooter_james_von_brunns_exwife_says_his_racism_ate_him_alive.html

Metapedia (2009). Barack Obama birth controversy. Retrieved August 12, 2009 from http://en.metapedia.org/wiki/Barack_Obama_birth_controversy

Mock, B. (2007). Sharing the hate: Video-sharing websites become extremist venue. Retrieved July 20, 2009, from
http://www.splcenter.org/intel/intelreport/article.jsp?ai
d=756

Miller, K. (2005). *Communication theories: Perspectives, processes, and
contexts.* New York, NY: McGraw-Hill Companies, Inc.

National Alliance (2009). Retrieved September 1, 2009 from
http://www.natvan.com/

National Socialist Movement (2009). Retrieved June 20, 2009,
from http://www.nsm88.org/

National Socialist Movement (2009). Tactics. Retrieved on June
22, 2009, from
http://www.adl.org/Learn/Ext_US/nsm/tactics.asp?L
EARN_Cat=Extremism&LEARN_S   ub-
Cat=Extremism_in_America&xpicked=3&item=nsm

National Socialist Movement (2009). Why you should join the
NSM? Retrieved on September 13, 2009 from
http://www.nsm88.org/articles/whyyoushouldjointhens
m.htm

New Saxon (2009). An online community for whites by whites.
Retrieved June 20, 2009, from http://newsaxon.org/

New Saxon (2009). Forum. Retrieved September 12, 2009 from
http://newsaxon.org/public/forum/topics/id_1/title_G
eneral/page_7/

Noelle-Neumann, E. (1991). Spiral of silence theory. In Katherine Miller's 2005 *Communication Theories: Perspectives, Processes, and Contexts.* New York, NY: McGraw-Hill Companies, Inc.

On the Verge of Civil War in America? (2009) Retrieved September 17, 2009 from
http://www.stormfront.org/forum/showthread.php?t=6
26602

Pew Center for Civic Journalism (2009). Retrieved October 12, 2009, from http://www.pewcenter.org/Podblanc (2009). Video Uploads. Retrieved August 15, 2009 from http://podblanc.com

Potok, M. (2008). Books on the right. Retrieved on August 20, 2009, from http://www.splcenter.org/intel/intelreport/article.jsp?ai d=904

Rabkin, J. (2000). Philosophizing public opinion. *Public Interest, 14,* 120-125.

Republican chairmen apologize for Jew remark (2009). Retrieved October 22, 2009, from http://www.msnbc.msn.com/id/33406727/ns/politics-more_politics/

Rodman, G. (2008). *Mass media in a changing world: History, industry, controversy.* New York: McGraw-Hill, 141.

Rolef, S.H. (Ed.). (1993). *Political dictionary of the state of Israel.* Jerusalem, Israel: The Jerusalem Publishing House Ltd.

Samoriski, J. (2002). *Issues in cyberspace: Communication, technology, law, and society on the Internet frontier.* Boston, MA: Allyn and Bacon.

Segel, B.W. (1995). *A lie and a libel: The history of the protocols of the elders of Zion.* Lincoln, NE: University of Nebraska Press.

Schein, E., Schneier, I., & Barker, C.H. (1961). *Coercive pressure.* New York: Norton.

Schweitzer, N.J. (2008). Wikipedia and psychology: Coverage of concepts and its use by undergraduate students. *Teaching of Psychology, 35,* 81-85.

Simi, P., & Futrell, R. (2006). Cyberculture and the endurance of white power activism. *Journal of Political and Military Sociology, 34:1,* 115-142.

Simon Wiesenthal Center (2009). Facebook, youtube+: How
    social media outlets impact digital Terrorism and hate.
    Produced by the Simon Wiesenthal Center & Snider So-
    cial Action Institute.

Shoemaker, P. (2003, November 20). Intercoder reliability. Re-
    trieved on March 10, 2007 from
            http://web.syr.edu/~snowshoe/content_analysi
    s/intercoder_reliability.doc

Shyles, L. (2003). *Deciphering cyberspace: Making the most of digital
    communication technology.* Thousand Oaks, CA: Sage Publi-
    cations.

Snow, D. A., Rochford, E. B. Jr., Worden, S. K., & Benford, R.
    D. (1986). Frame alignment processes, micromobiliza-
    tion, and movement participation. *American Sociological
    Review, 51:4,* 464-481.

Snyder, L.L. (1989). *Encyclopedia of the third reich.* New York, NY:
    Paragon House.

Southern Poverty Law Center (2009). About us. Retrieved Octo-
    ber 8, 2009 from
    http://www.splcenter.org/center/about.jsp

Steele, S. (1996). Taking a byte out of the first amendment. *Hu-
    man Rights: Journal of the Section of Individual Rights & Re-
    sponsibilities, 23:2,*14-22.

Stein, S. (2009). James Von Brunn apparently part of the
    "birther" movement. Retrieved June 25, 2009, from
    http://www.huffingtonpost.com/2009/06/10/james-
    von-brunn-apparentl_n_214006.html

Stormfront (2009). Retrieved May 15, 2009, from
    http://stormfront.org/forum/

Stormfront (2009). Forums. Retrieved September 8, 2009 from
    http://www.stormfront.org fo-
    rum/search.php?searchid=7917802

Supreme White Alliance (2009). Retrieved June 20, 2009, from http://swa43.com/drupal/

Swain, C.M., & Nieli, R. (2003). *Contemporary voices of white nationalism in America.* Cambridge, UK: Cambridge University Press.

Tactics for Recruiting Young People (2009). Retrieved September 2, 2009, from http://www.media-aware-ness.ca/english/issues/online_hate/tactic_recruit_young.cfm

Tapscott, D. (1998). *Growing up digital: the rise of the net generation,* New York: McGraw-Hill.

Tapscott, D. (2008). *Growing up digital: How the net generation is changing your world.* New York: McGraw-Hill.

Timothy McVeigh, Convicted Oklahoma City Bomber. (2001). Retrieved on August 12, 2009, from http://archives.cnn.com/2001/US/03/29/profile.mcveigh/

Top 100 Nationalists Websites (2009). Retrieved August 28, 2009, from http://www.ns88.org/index.php?a_m=1

Totilo, S. (2005), Racism among the many foes online gamers must fight. Retrieved on August 28, 2009, from http://www.mtv.com/news/articles/1514305/20051121/index.jhtml

United States Holocaust Memorial Museum (2002). Der Sturmer. *USHMM Propaganda Collection*: Gift of the Museum fur Deutsche Geschichte, Berlin.

United States Holocaust Memorial Museum (2009). In memoriam. Retrieved July 20, 2009, from http://www.ushmm.org/memoriam/detail.php?content=johns

Vanguard News Network (2009). Retrieved June, 2009, from
    http://www.vanguardnewsnetwork.com/

Viking Youth Corps (2009). Retrieved September 4, 2009 from
    http://www.nsm88.org/Youth/vycjoin.html

Volksfront (2009). Forum. Retrieved September 10, 2009 from
    http://www.volksfrontinternational.com/board/showth
    read.php?t=913

Weatherby, G.A., & Scroggins, B. (2006). A content analysis of
    persuasion techniques used on white supremacist web-
    sites. *Journal of Hate Studies, 4:9.*

Weigel, D. (2009). Scenes from the DC tea party. Retrieved Sep-
    tember 16, 2009 from
    http://washingtonindependent.com/38877/scenes-
    from-the-dc-tea-party-more-photos

Westboro Baptist Church: A publicity hungry-group (2009). Re-
    trieved on June 20, 2009, from
    http://www.adl.org/learn/ext_us/WBC/publicity.asp?
    LEARN_Cat=Extremism&LEARN_SubCat=Extremis
    m_in_America&xpicked=3&item=WBC

White Boy Society (2009). Retrieved on June 20, 2009, from
    http://localwhiteboy.com/home.php

White Boy Society Forums (2009). Retrieved September 17,
    2009 from
    http://www.whiteboysociety.net/e107_plugins/forum/f
    orum_viewtopic.php?1671

White Civil Rights (2009). Retrieved on September 9, 2009 from
    http://www.whitecivilrights.com/

White Nationalism (2007). Retrieved on June 20, 2009, from
    http://www.splcenter.org/intel/intelreport/article.jsp?ai
    d=863

White Supremacists and Anti-Semites Plan to Recruit at July 4
    Tea Parties (2009). Retrieved   October 1, 2009, from

http://www.adl.org/main_Extremism/White_Suprema
cists_July_4_Tea_Parties.htm

Women for Aryan Unity (2009). Retrieved August 24, 2009 from
http://wau14.com/

Yahoo search: Islamic (2009). Retrieved on August 20, 2009,
from
http://search.yahoo.com/search?p=Islam&ei=UTF-
8&fr=yfp-t-150&pstart=1&b=21

Young, K.S. (1996). Internet addiction: The emergence of a new
clinical disorder. *CyberPsychology & Behavior, 1,* 237-244

Zeskind, L. (2009). *Blood and politics: The history of the white nationalist
movement from the margins to the mainstream.* New York: Farrar, Straus and Giroux.

Index

About the Author

Adam Klein, Ph.D., is currently a visiting professor and teaching fellow at James Madison University in the School of Media Arts & Design. He received his Doctorate in Mass Communication & Media Studies from Howard University, and earned an M.F.A. in Screenwriting from the University of Miami. Adam is also a Sasakawa Young Leaders Fellow for proven research commitment to international conflict-resolution studies. Dr. Klein has published articles dealing with the topic of social movements and intercultural conflicts in the media, and has presented his research at several academic conferences including M.I.T.'s Media in Transition Conference in 2009, where this research debuted. As the grandson of two Holocaust survivors, Adam has focused much of his work on the present-day messages and messengers of hate speech and racial propaganda in the new global media.

CPSIA information can be obtained at www.ICGtesting.com

224047LV00001B/158/P

9 781936 117079